SEX, DEATH, AND OTHER DISTRACTIONS

ALSO BY
The Kensington Ladies' Erotica Society

LADIES' OWN EROTICA
LOOK HOMEWARD EROTICA

Sex, Death, and

Other Distractions

The Kensington Ladies' Erotica Society

ILLUSTRATED BY PAT ADLER

TEN SPEED PRESS
Berkeley / Toronto

1⊜
Ten Speed Press
P.O. Box 7123
Berkeley, California 94707
www.tenspeed.com

Distributed in Australia by Simon and Schuster Australia, in Canada by Ten Speed Press Canada, in New Zealand by Southern Publishers Group, in South Africa by Real Books, in Southeast Asia by Berkeley Books, and in the United Kingdom and Europe by Airlift Books.

Cover design: Jennifer Barry Design
Book design: Nancy Austin
Developmental editing: Melissa Stein

Any similarity to real persons, places, and events is in the eye of the beholder.

Library of Congress Cataloging-in-Publication Data on file with the publisher.

First printing, 2002
Printed in Canada

1 2 3 4 5 6 7 8 9 10 – 06 05 04 03 02

*To all the ones we've lost and miss
and will always love.*

CONTENTS

II. Objects and Desire

III. Flesh in Flux

IV. O Solo Mio

V. Ah, Men!

THE KENSINGTON LADIES
INVITE YOU IN

The Kensington Ladies are back! Older, yes; wiser, we wish. With all of us over sixty and a few over seventy, we are engaging in the hilarious struggle of growing old while still pursuing the joy of erotica in everyday life. We revel in the unexpected ways that arousal slips in and out of our shifting lives. In *Sex, Death, and Other Disctractions,* we want our readers to enter more rooms of our houses than just the bedrooms and to see more than the fantasy worlds that pre-occupied us when we embarked on this adventure twenty-five years ago.

For those of you who have never heard of us, the Kens-ington Ladies came together in the late seventies at the insti-gation of Sabina Sedgewick, who was then cataloguing a collection of erotica for the university library where she worked. With her fortieth birthday fast approaching, Sabina wondered if her lack of response was a portent of diminish-ing libido or simply a failure to relate to erotica written to titillate men. At a faculty party, she drew attention when she asked, "Do men and women agree on what is erotic?" She suggested that women should get together and explore the question. A stranger, Nell Port, slipped her card into Sabina's hand with "Call me if you get something going" scribbled on it. Sabina did.

We started reading Anais Nin, Henry Miller, Nancy Friday, *Penthouse,* and *Playgirl,* and shared our reactions over potluck dinners. Just as Sabina expected, none passed the arousal test. "Boring, too perfumed, masochistic," were the verdicts. That's when Sabina encouraged the group to write erotic fantasies of our own. We did—timidly at first, but with increasing relish as time went on.

Dashing off to our potluck dinners one night a month (after all domestic duties were done, of course), we fancied ourselves pioneers, staking a claim to a sexual life for older women. (Regarding our forties as "older" now makes us laugh until we howl.) We had only one rule: no victimization, which we agreed was decidedly unerotic.

After eight years of meeting, talking, laughing, crying, and writing, we had amassed quite a collection of stories, steamy and sweet, provocative, and, yes, sexy—at least to us. Only four of the then ten members wanted to submit the stories to a publisher. The rest were not interested. "Do it on your own time," they said. "We don't want to turn our meetings into work."

In 1984, with the publication of *Ladies' Own Erotica* about to become a reality, all of us suddenly balked at parading our fantasies in front of our sons and daughters and mothers and fathers, let alone total strangers. We quickly adopted pseudonyms and impulsively decided to wear masks for our book jacket photo.

The book catapulted to the top of the *San Francisco Chronicle*'s Bay Area bestseller list and was selected for the Quality Paperback Book Club. No one was more surprised by its success than the publisher, Ten Speed Press, for *Ladies' Own Erotica* violated every one of its publishing policies of the time: no fiction, no women's issues, no sex. So why did Ten Speed publish us? It seems that Phil Wood, Ten Speed's owner, sent the manuscript to cheer up Judd Boynton, a member of his board, who was hospitalized with advanced cancer. Boynton loved it, claimed it sent him into a remission, and wrote the production costs into his will to assure its publication.

Our second book, *Look Homeward Erotica,* published in 1986, carried on the success of *Ladies' Own,* but coincided with the alarming emergence of the AIDS epidemic. Sexual recreation lost its liberated high spirits as cautionary tales abounded.

We never envisioned writing another book. After spawning our second volume, we lay like spent salmon on the riverbank, gasping for breath. Wanting to ease into our remaining days as comfortably as possible, we were ready to toss our erotic remains back to the voracious young. We went our separate ways and met only for an occasional potluck reunion.

On one of these social evenings, sometime between the polenta and the clafoutis, Sabina raised the subject of our erotic lives. Most of us dodged the question, or tried to, until Sabina cut through our mumblings. "These days, I think a lot more about the deathbed than the marriage bed," she said flatly. The uneasy silence that followed told us she had hit a nerve, just as she had twenty-two years earlier when she had challenged us to divulge our middle-aged erotic longings.

We sprang to life, all speaking at once. In various ways, death was encroaching on all of us. Never in our years together had we talked to each other with such honesty. Recognizing that we were much closer to the end than to the middle, we suddenly felt we had no time to waste. One after another, we began to reveal our fears, denials, and secret bargains with the Grim Reaper. Sex and death have always been sparring partners, and in our different ways each of us was preparing to enter the ring. Suddenly, real life seemed much more compelling than sexy smoke and mirrors. By the time dinner was over, we had jettisoned the idea of masks and pseudonyms and were high on realism and self-revelation. We were going to bare it all!

We soon discovered that truth can be wilder than fantasy, but it exacts a price. We didn't want to hurt the people in our lives or dwell upon ailments and dustballs.

"I want my mask back!" said Susan.

"I need my pseudonym!" cried Nell.

"Me, too!" said Elvira. We dove for our disguises and were off, as flushed and reckless as before. Laughter returned to the dining room table and the Grim Reaper came out from the shadows only long enough to join us for a little dessert.

I. For Play

Now we were free to play. Nothing is more essential to an erotic life, whether real or imagined, than a sense of fun. Some of the Ladies revisited characters from earlier fantasies, reviving old lusts and finding more satisfaction than before, while others took new lovers. For those of us who had been "good girls" too long, it was a great relief to throw off the strictures of convention and to transport ourselves to the riskier edges of romance. We were invigorated to be thinking about erotica again and to be examining wantonness in the bright light of our computer monitors.

In this section, two faithful wives toy with the idea of adultery while another consummates a dormant romance with her high school sweetheart. Two other Ladies, each with a strong sense of place, wickedly ply their mischief in a hotel's presidential suite and in a dentist's waiting room.

These days, when our computers remember far more than we can, we find that we invent much faster than we forget. The group acts as a shock absorber for our uncensored blurts, and our loud hilarity scares away inner critics and outside editors. As one of our daughters observed, "You're lucky. You're at that age when you can say and do anything—at least in front of each other."

1

Natural Selection

ℰ ROSE SOLOMON

We are married, but not to each other. We met only two nights ago over dinner and laughter at a neighbor's lakeside cabin. Your wife, who stayed at work in a coveted position in a sweltering Eastern city, is probably relieved to have you out West visiting your old college roommate. Our attraction, sparked by friends in common and by a rapport that no one else seemed to notice, highjacks my thoughts and caffeinates my actions.

I think it started the moment we were introduced and your gaze held mine. I took in your blue eyes, white hair, smooth rosy skin. Funny, I thought, I don't usually linger on such Irish looks, but you seemed so fresh and eager. A suppressed smile played at the corners of your mouth, a sensitive, lively mouth with ready lips. I glanced away first, feeling your laser gaze burnish my cheek, neck, and shoulder, and immediately forgot your name. You offered me a beer and walked to the kitchen, away from me. I watched. You moved with grace, relaxed and leggy, light on your feet even though you are broader and heavier than I am used to. The hair at your neckline curled up slightly, soft as duck down.

The glass you handed me was cold, but it was your body

heat from a foot away that made me shiver. Your eyes crinkled
in a smile. You laughed easily, heartily. You weren't afraid
to be funny and self-revealing. When your old roommate
and his wife, who married right after college, teased you,
leeringly, about your womanizing past, you recalled their
"dishonorable mentions" with obvious, almost wondrous,
affection, "Yeah, that was Doreen. Wasn't she sweet? I really
fell for her. I think she became a pilot. And Laura, the
photojournalist? What a daredevil. She really raked me over
the coals."

I wondered how long ago that was and why it should
intrigue me. I usually shun womanizers. They are too narcis-
sistic and predatory to mess with. But all I could see in you
that night was evidence of a kind and open heart. You didn't
respond to your friends' lascivious ribbing, except to defend
the women they paraded from the past. It was clear to me
then that you love women, and I found that hugely appealing.
I watched you tune in and listen to others with such empathy,
Clintonian empathy, that I could imagine you wearing down
all resistance and earning complete forgiveness. Though you
engaged everyone, I came away thinking you especially liked
my jokes. You still refer to things I said that night. You make
me feel memorable. That is intoxicating.

Throughout that evening I watched my husband. Could
he detect my attraction for you? But he seldom looked my
way, and when he did, his eyes skated over mine, never really
stopping. When I spoke, I noticed him turn away and start a
conversation of his own with someone else. Sometimes I
tried to tune in, but the themes were too familiar and imper-
sonal to hold me for long: safe talk about travel and fishing.

Your friend and my husband, both avid fishermen, began planning a trip for the next day. You wearied of the fishing talk, turned, and asked if I was going with them.

"No, I don't fish."

"Neither do I. What do you do? Tennis, golf?"

"God, no!" I laughed. "I hate organized activity. Tennis courts are prisons—all that chain-link fencing and cruel scorekeeping. And golf is ridiculous—too much overfed, manicured grass and silly sportswear."

Your laughter egged me on, but I noticed a blush rising and realized you probably love golf.

"Oh no. Are you one of those Southern country club types?"

"Yeah, what are you?"

"A mountain woman, a nature girl. I don't do games that require balls and scores. I love wilderness."

Your smile faded into contemplation as you studied me.

"Show me," you said, your eyes on mine.

"What? Wilderness? My true nature?"

"Yeah."

I averted my gaze, too tempted for comfort. Thirty-four years of steadfast marriage had taught me to keep my wayward lust under wraps, to be content with what I already have—a kind husband, satisfying work. But as much as I value the simple life and the fragility of trust, your interest stirred some long-buried impulse. I wanted risk, not safety, and the rush of spontaneity over restraint. What would be the harm? With the kids launched, no chance of pregnancy, my parents buried, and my husband so hooked on fishing that he was beginning to think like a trout, no practicalities held me back. Besides, hadn't decades of good behavior earned me a day off?

Through the window behind your head I could see a faint halo of gold brightening the eastern horizon.

"Well, for starters, we could go watch that moonrise," I said, seizing the initiative.

We slipped away from the party without a thought and hurried through the woods to the lake for an unimpeded view. A bald, full moon crept over the rim of hill, spilling molten gold across the tar-black water. Down the beach a pier jutted out over the inky deep, and we climbed onto it, as if being two feet closer to the moon could make the spectacle any better.

It was cold standing at the end of the pier over the water, and I began to shiver, great squalls of shaking. You took off your sweater and pulled it over my head. The sleeves hung to my thighs, the shoulders almost to my elbows, and your residual warmth enveloped me extravagantly.

"You'll freeze!" I protested, and we pressed close, side to side, to salvage the warmth. I didn't dare take my eyes from the moon, so intent was I on absorbing this delicious moment. My head did not quite reach your shoulder. Your hip tucked against my lower ribs. Your arm enfolded me. I slipped one arm around your waist, an ample waist. You smelled faintly of something wild and woodsy, maybe bay or cinnamon. Neither of us said a word, just watched the ascending moon shrink from a yellow yolk and begin to harden into a cold, white disk. By then you were shivering, too, and we started to walk back to the party. I thought my knees would buckle from desire, so heady was the brew of cabled wool and body warmth and you. As we neared the cabin, I gave you back your sweater, feeling utterly and completely ravished.

The party was beginning to break up.

"So, how about a hike when they go fishing?" you asked, eagerly, as if we both were single and searching. "You be my guide?"

"I'll take you to my favorite lake. It's pretty far, so don't wear golf shoes with tassels."

   ⚭ ⚭ ⚭

Today the fates have tossed us a prize too good to refuse: a whole free day alone together. No one else knows where we are.

We are hiking in the Desolation Wilderness to my favorite alpine lake. It is set in granite like a misshapen topaz. There is an island in the lake that I want to swim to, and I have deliberately not brought a bathing suit. I wonder if that will make you uneasy, then catch myself: I am the one who is.

I've been anticipating this outing with too much gusto to pretend it's a Girl Scout picnic. I want to believe that your wife has little time or inclination to pamper you these days, leaving me the chance to spoil you. I'm glad I haven't met her; I would probably like her and a sisterhood of trust would develop, which I could never violate.

So I tell and retell myself that this is just a lark, one day out of our lives, a cliché really. It will be seamless: our loyalties are clear. We will both go home to our families. Your kids are younger than mine, two still in college. But for today I will play down these dear attachments and ratchet up my excitement.

I hope the sandwiches I've made will weave a spell. Will you fall for the turkey with pear-cranberry chutney or for the avocado with bacon and tomato? I want you to delight in the eating as much as I did in the planning. Will you like niçoise olives, salted edamame, peanut butter and celery, lemon cucumbers, and plump cashews as much as I do? Please understand, I'm striving for unanimous agreement, a boundless merging of mind, heart, and body.

Dessert, I think, should be eaten after our swim to the island: nectarines at the peak of juicy ripeness and muscat grapes. We will soak them in the cold water of the lake while we swim, and I will leave an unwrapped bar of bittersweet chocolate on a slab of granite to melt in the sun. We'll use it for fondue or body paint, depending on our whim.

The sky is cloudless. You comment on its deep cerulean blue, a color seldom seen in your lowland part of the country. The air, too, is unfamiliar to you. There is not a trace of humidity here in the Sierra high desert, and the unflinching sun warms the day to a perfect 82. Sweat evaporates before it forms.

Our boots crunch over the sundried pine needles that litter this part of the trail. Their fragrance is sweeter than childhood and takes me back to all the summers I spent exploring this terrain. Whenever I return I am six, eight, ten years old again—my ribs snug against a cotton T-shirt, my legs smooth against worn jeans. The soft air with its familiar summer smells brings back a riptide of tactile memories: the scent of the Sea and Ski that my cousins and I slathered onto each other's backs before baking on the splintery pier at our Truckee swimming hole; the sharp, minty pennyroyal that I rolled between my fingers while waiting for the boys to decide if I could come along on their hike; the acrid skunk cabbage that scraped our bare legs as we chased through a meadow in late August; the seedy tartness of thimbleberries that popped in our mouths; the citronella-soaked cottonball that hung above our beds on the sleeping porch to keep mosquitoes away. Deep in my heart nothing has changed.

Dipping back into childhood calms me. I gain the sense of cohesion I need to carry out this reckless adventure. We are the sum of all we have lived, I think, as I pick some stubby needles from a Douglas fir that's younger than I am even though it's twice as tall.

"This tangy resin spells summer for me," I say, handing the needles to you for your inspection.

I ask what your childhood summers smelled like. You remember honeysuckle and gardenia and swamp mud. You liked playing in dirt, too, damming up creeks. A Southern lilt creeps back into your voice as you remember. I think how far we have come, how much has accrued since then. We have weathered losses and disappointments and survived successes. Yet there is no other age I would want us to be. Who we are now feels solid and true, especially in this enduring landscape. I take your hand—bold, for this is something I haven't done before, actually reach out and touch you—and lead you to a Jeffrey pine.

"Close your eyes and sniff the trunk. Can you name the smell?"

Clearly a willing player, you press against the jigsawed bark. "Butterscotch?" you guess. "Vanilla?"

"Yes, either."

I release your hand, to assure you that this can be a casual encounter, it doesn't have to be anything more. I tell myself you don't have to match my spiraling lust; after all, who could? But these rational thoughts don't still my racing heart. Your beautiful, oversized hand, with its long fingers and cushioned palm, tender and strong, has left its hot brand. I can feel it against the small of my back, against my breastbone, against the curve of my belly even though you are walking three paces behind me.

We come to a newly fallen tree, a huge pine that weeps sap. Your long legs clear the trunk easily, but I have to scramble up on top. You turn and reach for me with both hands to lower me down. I feel like a child, feather-light in your grasp, and know I will keep replaying this moment.

We stop talking. There seems to be no need. The many years lived with others provide a shortcut to intimacy. We fall into a humming rhythm together like a long married couple, you the generic husband, me the generic wife, but now with the possibility of being reincarnated for one day as lovers. Time is compressed and urgent, as it is for mayflies.

The trail dips into the shadows of a fir forest, then snakes up and over granite ledges back into bright sunlight. We bound ahead like mountain goats, our pace synchronous, not noticing the steepening ascent. Somehow, in this theater of rock, a lone white pine and a few junipers have gained toeholds. Somehow, nearing the close of my sixth decade, I have found my footing.

We crest a summit, and our lake lies sparkling below. We decide to walk cross-country across a sloping shelf of granite that ends in a flat, sunny ledge on the northern shore.

Off-trail we can walk side by side, and, as we make our descent, you take my hand in yours. I leave it there, enjoying how small it feels in yours. Swept up again in another simulation of childhood, I want your reassurance that what we are about to do will turn out all right.

"Do you think it's possible to love several people faithfully?" I ask.

"Well, it depends how you define faithfully."

"No, faithful is faithful. We all maintain so many kinds of loving commitments—to our children, our friends, our spouses. I'm thinking it's how you define love. If love stands only for monogamy, that seems to me the opposite of love."

"Huh?" You eye me quizzically.

"It's too constricting. I like to think that love in all its forms can expand the heart, not constrict it, and that sexual love replenishes the overall supply. Shouldn't love beget more love?"

You are smiling with an almost fatherly, well-of-course-what-else kind of look. You put your hand on the back of my neck and give an affectionate squeeze. Your quiet laughter silences me. We stop walking. You cup my face in both hands and kiss my forehead before you answer.

"It's a gift. Simple as that. Words will take us in circles. But I think we agree. I've always preferred a profligate heart to a stingy one."

"Yes, but I want to be profligate and faithful. Can't I have it both ways?"

We laugh and turn toward the lake, walking hand in hand.

"What are you afraid of?" you ask, raising my hand to your lips.

"Having the rest of my life fall apart. One false move and it'll all go to hell."

"Funny you should use that word. The other night you said you were an agnostic, who shuns organized religion!"

"And you, the church-going seducer!"

Your eyes taunt me as you kiss my fingers, and we amble on.

At the water's edge we prop our backpacks against a tree and drink from your canteen. I sit down on a sunny patch of grass and take off my boots and socks. You stretch out on your back perpendicular to me, pillowing your head on my thigh.

"I need your discipline," you say, taking my foot in your hand.

"No, it's cowardice. I can't bear to hurt the people I say I love."

"Ahhh, that's virtue." You massage my bare foot, and something tightens in my groin.

"It's deprivation, too. I compensate with fantasies."

My hands burrow through your springy hair, notably dense for a man your age. My fingers disappear and cradle your skull. I want to trace the contours of your face—the strong jaw, the bumpy nose and brow ridge, the perfect fit of your ears against your head. I want to lean over and kiss you. I want to feel your skin and watch you undress. Are you hairy or smooth? Firm or flabby? On some level I think I already know, and whatever the condition of the goods, I want them all, no holding back.

"I'm generally a great sublimator," I say, "but I'm finding it harder and harder to resist you—here, now."

11

"Tell me a fantasy."

"All right, but let's eat while I do. I'm starving."

We sit cross-legged and spread the picnic between us. You are as enthusiastic as I'd hoped you'd be, and you surprise me with contributions of your own: Italian salami, the best white Cheddar I've ever tasted, Bing cherries, and macaroons. You've been anticipating this adventure, too.

"I like to fantasize about that island," I begin. "I know it's trite, but deserted islands spark my imagination. Where else can you be more free, more secluded, away from all distractions, no phones, no TV? Ever since I swam out there with a friend two summers ago, I've been imagining what it would be like to return with a lover. I see us hiding our clothes under a rock and diving in from this ledge."

"Ooooph!" You shudder.

"It'll be exciting, that sudden shock of cold, and if you swim without stirring up the water too much, you'll find warm spots. It takes about ten minutes to get there. We'll slither up onto those big, sun-baked boulders and lie side by side tingling in the sun, the wet hairs on our bodies standing on end like quills, our glistening bodies all hard and shivering, our fannies as firm and round as teenagers'.

"Once we warm up, we'll wander around our island Eden like Adam and Eve. We'll find shelter under those fir trees or maybe a cave in the boulders. Around the point is a beach nestled in a cove and a sunny meadow covered with shooting stars. There won't be any mosquitoes. We'll sit down in the grass facing each other...my legs over yours..."

"Wait, wait! Whoa! You've skipped some things, crucial

12

things," you say, propping yourself up on your elbow. "Scoot down here beside me while I fill in. First, we lie together, holding each other, like this. Rest your head on my arm so we can relax, face to face. I smooth your hair back, and your smile gives me the green light. I get to run my hand over your shoulder and shoulder blade, down your back, and over the curve of your hip, like this. I love that bone, the way it juts out. You press against me, yes, yes! And your hands can stay in my hair the way you were doing that's so nice. And we get to kiss…"

Your lips brush my cheek, kiss my nose and other cheek before settling briefly on my expectant mouth. I am laughing now, hoping you will stay, but you resume your story.

"You left that out. You're going to have to kiss me a lot if you want me to jump into that lake after you. Slow, steamy kisses like this…"

My toes curl as our mouths finally have their silent say and embark on explorations of their own. You are delicious—sweet and salty both. You take your time. You don't have an island to get to as I do. You are here, now. I am veering off course. My timetable is a shambles. You kiss my ear, and the voltage goes straight to my gut. My hands find their way under your shirt.

"Aaah," you say with a shudder, "yes! You glossed over this. You didn't undress us enough. I want to see what you're wearing under this tight little T-shirt. I want to see what kind of panties under your jeans. I want to see your skin…your breasts…your nipples, warm now in the sun…" Your big, gentle hands come together and cover them.

You caress me with slow, craving care. At one delirious point you tell me I am "so new," which makes me roar with laughter.

"I'm old! I've never been so old!" But I know exactly what you mean. We are completely new to each other, and nothing competes with the thrill of that.

          ⨧   ⨧   ⨧

You never did finish your story, at least not with words. Thought blurred into action. Now I replay the silent scenes with their subtitles of touch. Your solid presence grounded and freed me from the anticipation of what was going to happen next. Time fell away. Our only destination was the here and now. I was with you, over you, under you. We never did swim to that island. Instead, I freed you from the incarceration of your jeans. We made a nest of clothes. You folded your fleece jacket and placed it under my head. You lay over me, eclipsing the sun. I remember it as a cosmic event.

Back home now, I feel more alive in a jangled sort of way. I waken restless in the night and listen to my husband's gentle breathing. I try to imagine how your electrifying bulk would feel in this bed beside me. Would it ever become as safe and habitual as his? I wonder if you wake up, too, with disquieting thoughts like mine.

I am caught in a time warp, tripping between past and future. The present gets lost in the shuffle. When I try to remember how you slowed me down, I am back in the past. One day was not enough, no matter how many times I relive it. I daydream of meeting you again someday in a dozen different settings and find myself hurtling ahead, skipping over this moment, wanting more and more future moments with you. I am seldom here, now.

You send me two Bach CDs with a dried gardenia pressed between, and when I listen to them, I am with you again. I carry you along in my thoughts like a secret charm, certain that love, like the universe, keeps on expanding.

Today I mail you a flat, polished river stone small enough to carry in your pocket. It is black and smooth with an indentation on one side that I think will fit your thumb perfectly. I wanted to write that it's to bring you luck in everything you wish for, but then I caught myself catapulting you out of the present and into the restless future. Instead I wrote, "For now."

Bad Girls Do

&‎ NELL PORT

It's our fortieth high school reunion. It's not 1956, but *I'm* fifty-six. My high school love has dinner with me and my mom, and we reminisce about the good old days and catch up on some of the friends we had in common. He's kept in touch with everyone better than I have, and so I learn about marriages, divorces, and deaths of people I last saw when they were teenagers.

The pheromones are still alive and well; my sense of smell has a powerful memory. After dinner I walk him to his car, and we stroll up and down the block under a moonlit canopy of sycamore trees. We walk slowly, with our arms around each other's waists, and our footsteps in synch. At his car, he leans down and kisses me full on the lips, and the powerful sensations and memories come flooding back. I nestle into his sweater, and I feel sixteen again. My mother calls for me—worried, I think, that something sexual may be going on. We make plans to see each other the next day.

It dawns bright and clear, and I tell Mom I'm meeting an old girlfriend for a day at the beach. Filled with anticipation, I shower and wash my hair. I'm all tingly with the forbidden-ness of this tryst—after all, we're both married and have several children between us—but we both know exactly what we're doing. So I do head for the beach and a lovely old hotel overlooking the ocean, where we've agreed to meet. He's already checked us in, so I go straight up to our room. There's lunch, which we eat with gusto. He tells me how painful it was for him during all those years in high school, when we would spend endless hours necking and petting, but no more than that. Lily Tomlin refers to the fifties as a whole decade of foreplay, and for me it pretty much was. He tells me how much he wanted me but he also respected my wishes. I tell him how much I loved every bit of it, but I do feel a sense of unfinished business. I say that I want us to have a long session, just like we used to, but end it differently this time.

And so we go out on the balcony and melt into each other's arms. Our clothes come off in the same order as before—my blouse, my bra—but this time my knickers come off, too. And then he sheds his clothes, so we are both bare naked in the sun. Oh, the great luxury of being an adult and having a bed to look forward to instead of the backseat of a car! But suddenly the "nice girl" in me starts feeling a little shy and worried that I'll regret this. She warns me that I may be endangering my marriage. My body has a mind of its own, however, and it's not worried at all, even though it's certainly not the body it was forty years ago. So we fall onto the clean sheets and just hold each other tightly, letting the sensations fill us up and spill over. Now I'm fully in the moment, and I take the lead when I sense he is feeling overwhelmed. I see tears building up, and then I understand what this occasion means to him. It's the culmination of five years of our thwarted teenage lovemaking.

We go slowly, exploring all those long-ago familiar places. He always loved my breasts, so they get kissed and sucked and nuzzled first. I used to close my eyes right about now to create a distance, but this time my eyes are wide open, I'm right here, and there's that electric connection zapping straight down to my crotch! Then we venture into that less familiar territory, slowly, slowly, and with a dazzling acknowledgment that something we've both done thousands of times is somehow happening for the very first time. We look into each other's eyes as he enters me, and now it's mine that fill with tears. He rests inside of me and pulls me even closer. I remember well his tenderness, and his unwavering regard for my feelings. I tell myself that this act is my gift to him, but I realize that it is also his gift to me. Such a simple, natural act, yet I couldn't let myself "do it" for all those years. We move together, not so slowly now, and our orgasms— although not simultaneous—are perfect. They're each 250 orgasms all rolled up into one.

We laze about in each other's arms, laughing about why we couldn't have just done it back then. It's so easy! I refresh his memory about my principles, my fears, my parents, and he remembers. We shower, get dressed, walk on the beach-so I'll have a little color to show my mother—and when it's time to go, we kiss for a very long time and agree that this was a once-in-a-lifetime event. We'll hold onto the memory.

Then, holding hands, we run whooping and laughing across the sand back to our room.

Hors d'Oeuvres: A Recipe

✧ BERNADETTE VAUGHAN

For the Ladies, hors d'oeuvres have always been magical. They signal the witching hour, the time of withdrawal from the world, when we prepare to slip down what are still, even after all this time, the virgin passages of our imaginations into the wine-dark seas of erotic fantasy. The ritual never changes: we wash the grapes, unwrap the Camembert, slice the baguettes, sample the olives, and hunt through the Lady of the Night's cupboards for the bowl or platter that will best present the tempting morsels we have brought, calculated to sharpen our senses and prepare us for the feast to come. We pull from our baskets and bookbags the stories and poems that will be our compass, as night falls, for the enchanted journey and set them aside to read aloud over dessert. Then, seated around the coffee table, we pour the gold and ruby wine, snap open the bubbling water and turn our attention to the food.

Over the years, we've cooked enough dinners to earn us an E for Enough in a collective *cordon bleu*. So, sometimes, the hors d'oeuvres *are* dinner. Once ensconced around the coffee table, we do not get up. We recline, shoes off, leaning languidly into soft cushions. We eat with our fingers, licking silky aioli from the underside of pâté-laden flatbread, care-lessly wiping oil spills from the front of a shirt. In the sum-mer, tiny red, yellow, purple, and orange tomatoes burst against the roofs of our mouths in sweet candy spasms, liq-uefying the love-bite of the white Maui onions. In the winter, brooding and recumbent, sticky Medjool dates succumb to the creamy, insistent effluence of the Brie across the cheese-board.

The following recipe is one of my all-time favorites, as it is absurdly simple and serves large numbers of people with minimal effort. It combines goat cheese (the rank, raunchy kind that comes, you would swear, with bits of the barn floor still sticking to it and a shuddering, hormone-charged aroma that calls up the lewd, yellow-slitted gaze the billy goat bends upon his harem) with the dusky lusciousness of purple-black Mission figs, served warm.

BERNADETTE'S BAKED FIGS
STUFFED WITH CHÈVRE

> Preheat the oven to 365 degrees. Now select plump black figs, allowing three to four per person, at that stage of ripeness when they are on the verge of spilling their seeds but not quite bursting from their skins. Reject any chewy ones. Wash the figs gently and disperse them on a clean dish towel. While they are drying, remove the goat cheese from the refrigerator and, while it is still stiff, cut slices that would slightly overflow a teaspoon. You need double the number of slices as figs. Lightly spray a shallow, ovenproof dish—preferably one that can go directly to the table—with olive oil and set it aside. Now cut each fig in half. Place

a knob of cheese on each half and arrange the fruit in the baking dish. Bake for ten to twelve minutes, until the figs and the cheese are moistly fused, and serve straight from the oven. For exquisite pleasure this preparation is best eaten with the fingers, so have a generous supply of napkins on hand and perhaps some finger bowls filled with rose–petal scented water at body temperature.

Farewell to the President

 ∾ SABINA SEDGEWICK

Not even a mouse could find a hole that the Secret Service hasn't searched with high-tech gear and special-agent eyes. Yet they don't see that I have replaced the hideous hotel bouquet with a branch of cherry blossoms coaxed into full bloom in my sunny kitchen window. They'll never smell the Armani cologne I've sprinkled on the pillows, nor the subtle aroma of sage oil (for wisdom) and lavender (for relaxation) that I've rubbed around the marble tub, basins, and floor—genuine Carrara marble that makes the bathroom look like a Renaissance tomb. They don't give a damn if the cleaners douse it with Clorox and Pine-Sol. Me they wave away like a speck of dust. It's not just my dust-gray maid's uniform, but the way I look. Eminently forgettable.

But not to him.

He gives me that special wink as he passes me in the corridor, where I've flattened myself against the wall. Now I only have to wait for his entourage to leave him alone. When they come out, they look right through me. To them I'm just a stack of towels going into the president's suite.

He's stretched out on the bed, fully clothed, his long legs flopped beyond the rose and blue-striped coverlet. The colors are identical to the ones on the Oval Office couch. He keeps his eyes closed as I take off his boat-sized shoes and gently massage the ball of his right foot. We both have jobs that require us to be constantly on our feet. But that roguish smile around his lips tells me that he's awake and waiting for more than a foot massage.

I crouch down on the bed, next to his hips—those narrow, long hips I've memorized—and unclasp the silver buckle with the presidential seal. He sighs. Instead of the zipper, I reach for the pleasing plumpness underneath his pants as if I was cuddling a kitten out of its hiding place. Then taking time before releasing my present, I dip my tongue through the zipper's spread teeth, testing and teasing the silky ridge inch by inch. The official charcoal gray of his pants sets off the humor of his candy-striped boxer shorts. Fixing my eyes on the fully risen glory, I genuflect before the most powerful man in the world. I am in awe of how vulnerable a man is, with his privates in a woman's mouth. And if he is the president, he risks everything. I could betray him to his enemies, I could be a spy. I know everything about him. Yet he has no idea who I really am underneath my uniform— I doubt he could even describe my face. I am a professional, proud of my natural inclination for being discreet. Seeing him lying in front of me, totally exposed, I feel humbled by his trust and enormously aroused.

Today I can hardly resist my impulse to guide his missile to my crotch. But my sense for what is appropriate prevails. After all, I am a maid. I know that intimacy must have limits, especially when handling a president. Within these limits, which I have set myself, we are free to serve our pleasure.

To desire what we can get and give is much more gratifying than to dream. That's also true for politics, I think. I think it's the secret of success for maids and presidents.

For that reason, my delight of choice is to sip from the presidential power spring. My lips enfold his tumescent spout, my cheeks yield to its tender toughness. We gasp together as he squirts his man-juice on my tongue.

I wonder if he knows that I've served him to satisfy my own appetite. It is I who am fastidious about sensual ambience. The perfumes I have squirreled away from other suites mean nothing to him. I need my erotic props, my costume. That's why I spend hours setting the stage, while the performance is necessarily short. Brief, intense, risky, and in my control. That's how I like it. And so does he. We're a match.

Once we leave this room, our lives divide in opposite directions. It's always a great comfort and honor when he says that he hates to leave me. This is my signal to disappear as unobtrusively as I came. I am used to hurried departures. But today is his last trip here before he leaves office. Maybe I'm hoping to hear something different, although I can't think of anything that would dispel my sadness over our parting after all these years. I'm quite startled when he suddenly bounces from the bed pulling me up next to him.

"As far as I know, ex-presidents still have access to this suite," he exclaims happily.

I could kiss him smack on the lips for his sexy grin. Luckily I have his speeches on videotape so that I can admire him all I want.

But how can I explain to him that his scheme won't

work? The ego of the president is as big as his penis and as vulnerable. So I stay as unobtrusive as the air he breathes, and as essential. But maybe he of all presidents will find it amusing if I confess my passion? As long as I choose my words carefully. "Mr. President," I hear myself speak with the modesty becoming to a maid, "I will always remember you. But I'd spoil my experience with you when you were president if I repeated it when you're an ex." No, that would be cruel. It will be difficult enough to get used to being an ex without me revealing that my taste is exclusively for presidents in office.

So I make my farewell as diplomatic as I can. "I think of you like a fine wine, Mr. President. How well I remember the difference between your first and fourth year. From raw and robust like a Beaujolais Nouveau you matured to sassy, earthy, yet slightly sweet; then, in your fourth year, you became sensual and intense like a Château Margaux. But your second term brought out your full-bodied complexity. Meaty, with a dramatic hint of pepper, you developed into a sensational blend of power and elegance. A vintage Château Lafite-Rothschild comes to mind, perhaps overpowering for some, but for me you achieved the balance of all the flavors in a truly great wine, while adding a daring, yeasty flavor, perfectly matched with a mellow creaminess. I'd rather practice abstinence than spoil the exquisite treat you gave me when you matured in this second term."

Of course I didn't say any of this. I just folded his bedspread like a flag for the departed hero, and presented it to him with a slight bow and a geisha-like smile.

"What's this?" he asked looking confused.

"A souvenir. I wouldn't want this to get into the wrong hands," I said. "It was custom-made for you." I was already thinking about the new colors that might go with the next president. Something more traditional, of course, earth tones with a slick, black satin lining for Texas oil? Oops—I almost committed a faux pas. That pattern was already used.

He must have read my thoughts. "I guess you're ready to make up the bed for my successor?" His intuition is almost psychic.

At that moment, I realized how much I'd miss the man, the way he laughs a real belly laugh as he opens the door and turns the card around to "Maid Service, please."

Laughing Gas

ॐ ELVIRA PEARSON

When the couple walked into the lobby of my dentist's office, I hardly looked up. I had been thumbing through *Runners' World,* waiting for the hygienist to call my name. I soon became aware that the male member of the couple was here for one of those mildly terrifying surgical procedures, for he was the one who walked briskly to the receptionist's counter and announced his presence while she sauntered over to the drab gray upholstered chairs where I was seated. When given what I presumed to be a release form, I heard him say, with a quick laugh that was not a laugh at all, "These are all the horrible things that could happen, right?" I smiled, recalling my own reaction to such small-print warnings when I had dental surgery years ago. Knowing that I was there for a simple maintenance cleaning, I felt a surge of relief.

If I were to place his age, I would guess he was closing in on fifty. He was a bit on the disheveled side, and, from my furtive glances, I think he was wearing suspenders or hiking boots or heavy twill trousers with large outer pockets. At any rate, something evoked my romantic notion of a back-woodsman, albeit I have never known a "backwoodsman." I do recall that he had sandy hair, a nice flat tum-tum, and was of average height. Except for his dress, in fact, one might say he was nondescript, in the way the character actor William H. Macy is nondescript. (Having been raised on Hollywood movies, actors are deeply woven into my sensibilities. I always thought of my aunt and uncle as Jeannette McDonald and Nelson Eddy.)

As for her, I remember that she was fleshier than he, "fleshy" in the best sense of the word. (Kathleen Turner comes to mind.) She was wearing an oversized white cotton shirt and a long black skirt. Having glanced at them frequently enough to feel a little uncomfortable, I returned to *Runners' World.* It was then that I heard him say to the receptionist,"I wonder if someone would call my wife about a half hour before I'm through here so she can pick me up." Jolted out of my easy assumptions, I stopped to reckon with this new detail: the woman with him was not his wife—and clearly not his daughter, either.

When he had finished his check-in, the man walked over to where his friend, whoever she was, was now seated. Immediately and animatedly, he started to whisper to her and she to him. I strained to pick out words and sentence fragments before chastising myself and going back to my desultory reading. But as I flipped pages, my attention strayed to the low, vibrant buzz of conversation just three feet away. I looked up at the exact moment when she reached for his hand and clasped it in hers. Just before I averted my eyes, she stood up, faced him, leaned forward, and kissed him full on the mouth. A whispered goodbye, and she left.

He immediately closed his eyes and seemed to sink into a kind of meditative state. Perhaps he was preparing for the coming ordeal. On the other hand, I mused, he might be reliving an afternoon tryst, one that he and his Kathleen had carefully, playfully, arranged to concoct a few lusty memories for him to replay as the dentist unceremoniously invaded his mouth.

I closed my eyes and heard her say, "They'll give you something to make you drowsy, darling; just let yourself drift off into la-la land." How he must have loved the soft growl of her voice that made "pick me up at my apartment" sound like "bury your warm fingers in my crotch." I could see a sly, there-there smile spread over her face as she gently slipped the suspenders from his shoulders. Images and dialogue began to tumble all around me. She proceeded to unbutton him everywhere, smiling all the while. As she undid the tiny hidden buttons of his fly, she looked straight into his eyes and whispered, "You are my darling buttonfly." The image made her laugh as heartily as if someone else had said it.

I saw him smile mischievously as he slipped his hands inside her open shirt, deftly undoing the clasp that kept her full breasts bound and letting his hands roam gently over her flesh, his thumbs caressing her aroused nipples. A lesser talent would have yanked at the fabric that stood between him and the familiar warmth of her skin, but he had obviously cultivated a "slow hand." She closed her eyes for a second to savor the myriad sensations looping their way through her body—now sharp, darting, and electric, now slow, liquid, and thick.

His trousers, held on by a thick woven belt, had not yet fallen to the floor, although his wild friend had escaped through his open fly, and was now standing at attention. As she stopped to quickly push her long skirt down over her hips, taking her underpants along for the ride, he seized the moment to undo his belt. She pushed her body against him, edging forward and forcing him to the wall. The heat of her pressed into him like a heavy blanket warmed in the sun.

Placing her hands on each side of his face, she began kissing him, lightly at first and then deeply. She rubbed her cheek against his and then put her tongue to his ear to tease the inner cavity, withdrawing from time to time to whisper. (What was she saying? Her voice had dropped to a low purring sound and I could barely make out her words.) "Do that little thing you do…you know. Do it. Oh, god, yes." He cupped his hands around her buttocks and pulled her toward him, his eager friend now straining to hold himself in check. Half leaning against the wall, they clung together, now breathing hard, when…

"Ms. Pearson?" Startled, I placed *Runners' World* back on the table, and followed my hygienist without a backward glance.

Viaticum

& BERNADETTE VAUGHAN

It is a warm day in late August and Mrs. Hollyholmes
sits under a gingko tree at a sidewalk cafe table. In the distance, open and unfolded, the platinum beach sighs its enrap-
tured response to the Pacific's caresses, drawing the foaming
surges into its hot embrace, clinging, then reluctantly releasing them. Mrs. Hollyholmes tucks an unruly white/blond
curl behind her ear and sighs in unison. She inhales the salty,
female scent of the ocean; her exhalation has the gravity, the
aroma, of the delicate, ozone-laced breeze that brushes her
bare skin and ruffles her hair.

She has been observing the way the light falls upon the
objects on the table before her, underscoring the "it-ness of
things" that these days (though she cannot place the quota-
tion) grabs her attention and renders her momentarily mute.
Her champagne flute, a faint smudge of lipstick gleaming at
its rim, its sparkling contents still registering the pop and fizz
of an exiting cork. The half-eaten crab cakes, flecked with
saffron, strewn across the coppery-green glisten of mesclun
on her pushed-aside plate. The butter melting in its bowl; the
scraps of croissant jeweled with preserved strawberries; the
fruit and the flowers and the heavy hotel-style tabletop

appointments, large knives and forks and spoons whose heft and luster take her breathlessly back to her childhood in France, when her daily task was to set the table for the serious, midday family meal. The gold glint of her wedding ring, which she wears, European fashion, on her right hand, and the pale pearl polish of her exquisitely manicured nails. The curve of her wrist—the freckled skin prominently mapped with blue veins whose color exactly matches the square-cut aquamarine winking in the ring she bought on her husband's behalf for her sixty-fifth birthday—that rests on the cast-iron table, inches from the tanned male hand she shook not an hour ago, when she was introduced. Friend of a friend, meet friend of a friend. Somehow, they have ended up sitting next to each other, expatriate Europeans decorously discovering interests in common. She has learned that he grew up in Brussels, now lives in Montreal, and is staying with friends in town for a few days on his way to Vancouver on business.

It seems to Mrs. Hollyholmes that the air between her hand and that alien male hand is textured and aware, as if an invisible intention has fashioned from the ether a velvet line that has snaked out, binding their proximity. For there is no mistaking—even at this late stage in the game, for he must be well into his seventies—the attraction that flared between them at the outset and that Mrs. Hollyholmes, an attractive woman, chic and lithe and what her mother would have called "well preserved," who in the course of a vivacious social life meets many men of her own age, was too startled, or perhaps too fatigued, to evade, much less ignore. As ordinarily she would: she often sees interest light men's eyes and habitually responds by vacating the psychic moment, by gracefully, almost imperceptibly, slipping through an invisible door and vanishing without announcing her departure. The art of being physically present and psychically missing has its own technique and Mrs. Hollyholmes has perfected it, for by and large she does not like men of her own age. She belongs to the last generation of pre-liberated women and likes to think that she is open-minded and tolerant—after all, it's not really their fault, poor lambs, how could it be? They were badly brought up and old habits, instilled by expectation and training and reinforced by practice and reward, die hard— but her observations have persuaded her that, the heady aphrodisiacs power, wealth, and fame notwithstanding, after the age of sixty they are more trouble than they are worth. They are, in a word, tiresome, being riddled with the sort of psychopathologies that either transfix them in mental permafrost (causing their often really quite impressive intellectual capacities to dwindle to dime size) or emotionally stunt them (rendering them impervious to new ideas) or reduce them to such lamentable states of physical disrepair that the entire interpersonal agenda dwindles to a single issue: the procurement of the nurse/cook/housekeeper/chauffeur who will keep things on an even keel until the Grim Reaper— upon the midnight, one hopes, and with no pain—swings his scythe and tosses them, frail and comatose, up in the great arc of his swath and sends them somersaulting through the suspended air, never to be heard from again except in remembered quotes.

And, of course, there is the matter of Mrs. Hollyholmes's ailing husband. Professor Hollyholmes ("Holl" to his colleagues and students, whose admiring legions stretch back through time), when it comes to defending his property, has in more robust times demonstrated the perspicacity of a clairvoyant, the hearing of a fruit bat, and the night vision of a great horned owl, combined with the heat-seeking attributes of a Smart Bomb and the instincts of a street-fighter. Mrs. Hollyholmes doubts that the energy he has mustered in the past in the deployment of any of these talents would be dissipated by his current situation, which is to say, flat on his back on a hospital bed with medical technology in all its fell battalions of drips and tubes, electrodes and oxygen monitoring every murmur, every beat, every twitch and gurgle, every minuscule surge in the most trivial of his body's mysteries.

No, the idea of an affair exhausts Mrs. Hollyholmes. She has said as much to her women friends, the ones she confides in, who have formed a sort of benign fifth-column (Holl calls it her coven) to give her the occasional weekend off, which is how she happens to be attending this party in the little oceanside town famous for its sexy septuagenarian moviestar mayor. They urge her, in the interests of survival in this bleak, extended time, to consider a dalliance. The suggestion has also been discreetly floated during meetings of her caregiver's group, which, being co-ed, might have its own agenda.

But Mrs. Hollyholmes demurs. She is a realist; she knows that adding the thrill and magic of extramarital romance to her life would cloud her vision. She would be at the mercy of her imagination, undone, launched into a dreamy world of fantasy that would wrench her feet from the clay she requires—probably has always required—to maintain her equilibrium. And think of all that subterfuge, all the lies and evasions, the drugstore purchases—the condoms, the lubricants, the inevitable Vagisil—to conceal; the phone calls to intercept; the appointment book to encode—her husband's idea of togetherness encompasses a very sketchy notion of privacy—so much work! On top of all the work his illness, his long, debilitating, repetitious illness, already exacts? Heaven forfend! She needs to lie down, she tells her friends, after merely entertaining the thought. They are persistent. Perhaps a long-distance affair, then, consummated every two or three years and conducted at a remove via airmail? She laughs lightly and brushes the topic aside; there are worse things, she says, than loneliness.

Besides, Mrs. Hollyholmes takes her marriage vows very seriously. *For better, for worse, in sickness and in health, forsaking all other 'til Death do us part.* Solemn, sonorous words, chilling and full of portent and not to be read flightily. Bonnets over the windmill, she believes, are simply not part of her repertoire. She was, after all, born in the first half of the last century and received what amounted to a late Victorian upbringing, her education, entrusted to Irish nuns in a rigid French order, markedly emphasizing duty and deportment. One does not, Mrs. Hollyholmes was taught and has always believed, betray one's vows. Not even if one's marriage turns out to be a poor return on investment, which Mrs. Hollyholmes, priding herself on an unflinching ability to call a spade a spade, acknowledges that by and large hers has revealed itself to be. Not that she is all that surprised. Mrs. Hollyholmes has always thought that marriage is rather like adopting a basically intelligent, and therefore easily rendered neurotic, animal—a dog, say, or a parrot—that has been abused or abandoned. There are too many unknowns;

there is simply no way of telling what murky traumata in the past have irrevocably degraded the ruminative pathways to the present. All one can do is wait and see and, having seen— well, make the best of it.

And she has taken them seriously.

Her vows.

Very seriously.

Until today, anyway.

Today, in the shade, at a cafe table on a sidewalk, with gulls wheeling and swooping overhead and otters, gleaming and sinuous, diving and surfacing among the glistening, swollen kelp, and the sun dripping like spilled white wine over every rooftop, surface, and tree, something is different. A stranger's shapely hand inches from her forearm is making her acutely aware of a silent, palpable resonance that reminds her of the shiver that runs through stroked crystal just before the release of the unearthly, piercing sound. The hand is square and muscular, attached to a finely wrought wrist that emerges from the rolled-back cuff of a dark blue linen shirt. The fingertips and thumb are spatulate, the nails are clipped, the hairs running along the back of the hand and up the forearm gleam like iron filings. Mrs. Hollyholmes stares thoughtfully at the hand, notices that it wears no wedding ring, watches as it moves to the ice bucket in the middle of the table, removes the champagne bottle, and refills her glass with the simple assumption that she would take as much pleasure in drinking another glass of wine as its owner would take in pouring it. Then, having replaced the bottle in the ice, the hand drops gently on hers and closes on her palm.

She feels his warmth on her cool skin and, slanting her

eyes to avoid turning her head—she has no intention of sig-
naling withdrawal—she notices that his left arm is draped
along the back of her chair, in that eloquent, adhesive gesture
that has always moved her, always elicited a silent gasp of
longing when she observed it, receiving, in a restaurant or at
a dinner party, like a thud in her side, the assured, telegraphed
acknowledgment of the coupled bond and, with it, the desolate recognition of deficit in her own relationship. Now,
fluidity rippling down her spine, feeling herself encircled,
feeling his fingers as they stroke the flesh of her upper arm
where it emerges from her sleeveless blouse, she knows she
wants more of what it is that the gesture, with all its subtlety,
signals. She leans in his direction and, since the table is small
and they are already in close proximity, she feels his body
heat enlivening the contours of her own, spilling over into
the silken vibrancy of her clothes against her skin, drenching
her. She has not worn these clothes before today, had wondered whether to buy the pale green skirt flaring at her
ankles, the slightly paler cropped chiffon top with the covered buttons, precisely because of the sleevelessness, for she
has a horror of being perceived as what was disparagingly
referred to in her youth as "mutton dressed up as lamb."
Usually, it is Holl, who has good taste and a discerning eye
for fabric and design, who is the final arbiter of her fashion
choices, but the day she saw the clothes in the window he
was already indisposed and in no position to offer a critique.
She went into the boutique and tried them on; they spoke to
her in the language of the body and she fell in love with
them. The silk had a heavy, suede-like texture that clung to
her hips and outlined her thighs as she walked up and down

the fitting room, loving the look of herself in the mirror, loving herself as graceful, sensual, desirable—*precious* was the word she finally chose. She charged them to her credit card and did not wear them to the hospital when she went to plant a goodbye kiss on Holl's pallid, barely sentient brow.

So here she is, Gem Hollyholmes, devoted wife and sole caregiver to an invalid husband, mother of four grown children now dispersed about the globe, leaning back, in full sight, into a strange man's discreet, but by no means furtive, embrace. She feels confused, but only mildly so; mostly she feels luxurious, languid, and very, very curious. She stirs and feels the questioning response in the hand that covers hers, the hesitancy in the hand at her shoulder, and she turns her head and meets his eyes. *Don't move away.* Is she sending the message, or receiving it? His eyes are hazel, rimmed with black—the lashes, the eyebrows that contrast sharply with his polished pewter hair—and she sees that the skin around them is webbed and crosshatched with diary lines. No part of his life, she thinks, no experience, no memory, has been allowed to become extinct. She catches her breath, recalling the pivotal center of her life as a young woman, the calm acceptance of herself as a glorious sexual force; how that unabashed certainty had enhanced her, hallowed her, as though her trajectory were traced in gold ink and filled in with colored crayon. How she loved it, back then, her power, her orgulous immersion in her own allure, her gaiety and skill as a partner in the rapturous dance—oh, the exhilaration, the fun of it all! How could she have let it evaporate?

Gently letting her fingers linger on his while releasing her

hand from the circle of his grasp, Mrs. Hollyholmes raises
her champagne glass to the man at her side and ponders the
notion of fun as essential provender for the soul's journey.
Her husband, she learned early in her marriage, is not committed to the concept. Her effervescence, so appealing during
the glowing days of courtship, exhumed in the harsher light
of marriage his buried fears of female waywardness and
betrayal, eliciting from him silent, but almost palpable,
dread. Dismayed, she quickly doused her flame. Theirs is—
has been—a life of grace and style and erudition, a lot of
erudition; whatever fun that filtered through has been of her
own making, involving the children, her circle of close
friends, her social contacts. Mrs. Hollyholmes is suddenly,
fiercely aware of her hunger for fun, for what Jacques Brel
described as *a few good times before it ends;* simultaneously,
she becomes aware that the hand that had been resting on her
shoulder now caresses the curve of her jaw, and she tilts her
head to the side in response, feeling his knuckles brush her
cheek. Together they watch the French accordionist who is
strolling among the tables, playing the *bal-musette* music
that she loves. Instinctively, her body engages the notes, her
need to respond suffusing her with excitement. It's been so
long since she danced, lightly, expertly, with a partner. Some
years ago, she suggested to Holl that they take lessons
together; it would be something for them to fall back on, she
reasoned, as their days shortened and conversation grew
sparse, the way it does in long marriages. She was astounded
by the withering scorn of his response. It was as though, she
confided to her friends, she had suggested something

unspeakably *louche*, like partner swapping, or rolling herself nude in Saran wrap for cocktails with the chair of a Ph.D. committee. She never raised the subject again, simply submitting to his resolute, heavy-footed, and exclusive propulsion of her body around the dance floor whenever social situations made a quickstep or cha-cha—oh, what earthly difference did it make, for heaven's sake, given the limits of his repertoire?—inevitable. She turns impulsively to the man at her side but he intercepts her.

"Dance with me," he says.

He stands up and holds out his hands and she moves into his embrace. They start to move and joyfully she realizes that he can do it; he is a European, so he can dance; he is a marvelous partner, graceful and strong and unafraid. He holds her with immense assurance, his hand firm on her back, guiding her, her hand light and soft in his, welcoming his direction as he welcomes her expertise. Waltz, tango, salsa, paso doble: it is as if they cannot stop. She follows his lead as they spin and sway between the tables, he looks down at her radiant, tilted face; she is ecstatic, saturated with music, she anticipates his moves, feeling the impulses that flow from his body, from his chest and arms and thighs, into hers. She thinks: I am dancing with the perfect partner, the most beautiful man in the world, and she wonders if this might be all there is of heaven.

But it is not, of course, because when the music ends they stand together under the ginkgo tree, still swaying, her hands clasped behind his head, his hands clasped at her waist, supporting her, their eyes *devouring*. Then, when the party is over, they walk down to the beach and take off their shoes and wander hand in hand at the water's edge, his trousers rolled up above his ankles, her skirt hem soaked, and watch the voluptuous rolling of the breakers and the crimson configuration of the sunset clouds piling up on the rim of the world. And then they pause and face each other and he takes her hand and raises it to his cheek, turning it over and kissing the palm as if its small area encompasses all the world and the breathless moment all of time, and then she slides into his arms and his hands move on her back, their exploring kisses begin, slow and unutterably delicious, their bodies and their beings saturated with desire. They release each other, pulling apart until only their fingertips touch, and find they cannot separate; aching and disheveled, they sink down in the shadow of a dune, his belt unbuckled, his shirt open to the navel, her skirt bunched around her waist, her bra unhooked; and they lie together on the deserted beach; they kiss again, explore again the wet smooth taut places, and the dry wrinkled loose places until he says he must leave, his hosts have invited friends for drinks in an hour especially to meet him, he must show up but he can bow out early, he is not committed for dinner, so perhaps, later, if she is free....

She sits between his bent knees on the sand, his hands on her breasts under the sleeveless, cropped top, hers caressing his knees, his thighs, and arches her back against his chest and leans her head into his shoulder as his mouth sweeps her neck. She thinks about the great soft bed in her hotel room with its view of the swelling ocean, and the long curtains blowing gently at the windows that lead out to the balcony, and how the moon riding low in the night sky lights a glittering path on the sea to the horizon, and how her marriage vows are distant shapes in her mind, irresolute and forlorn, like signposts swinging on their hinges and pointing in no particular direction.

"I am free," she tells him.

The Return of My Gardener

❧ ROSE SOLOMON

This year, on the fifth of April, to celebrate becoming a full-fledged sexagenarian, I treat myself to a day in the garden. I am squatting in a bed of Iceland poppies trying to spread a cubic yard of steer manure without decapitating the fragile flower heads. They bob on long, hairy necks like yellow, peach, pink, orange, and white balloons. The colors scream out in joyous contrast to the black-brown backdrop of manure. Piercingly pungent, it steams in the sunlight, drying out after a week of rain.

I weed and poke in the dirt as I go, and find a buried marrow bone. I toss it to Meeker, who watches from a bed he's dug in the ivy. The truffle tip of his long nose sniffs the bone, snorts, and lifts to scan the more telling currents of warm air. He is too dignified a custodian to be diverted by an old bone. His task is to watch me toil, maintaining his garden as it deserves to be kept. With his head still raised, he appraises me approvingly before closing his eyes in a half doze.

"Rose, is that you?" calls a white-haired man from the other side of the picket fence.

Meeker dashes to greet the stranger like long-lost family.

"Tomas!" I say. The soothing timbre of his voice is unmistakable. "My God, it's you!"

I step carefully out of the poppy bed and run to the fence. We hug exuberantly from opposite sides of the barrier, ignoring the pickets that jab our ribs. Meeker, standing on hind feet, presses and licks his way between us.

"This couldn't be Clyde," says Tomas.

"No, it's Meeker. He's our third dog since you left. God, how long has it been?" I ask.

"Nearly twenty-five years. I met you in September 1976."

"You remember," I laugh. "Just look at us. White hair! Are we old?"

"You're in great shape," he says.

"Must be all the gardening, and yoga."

"That's what I need," says Tomas. "Who's your gardener now?"

"Me."

"You? Just you?"

"Mostly, except for tree trimmers. The older I get, the more I love physical work. I'm trying to be an eighteen-year-old boy. Come on in and see what I've done."

Tomas laughs and enters through the gate, fastening it behind him as meticulously as ever. He doesn't tower over me the way I've remembered him, maybe because the work shoes are on the other foot now. I'm wearing high clogs, and he's the one in sneakers. He's thinner and a bit stooped.

"Didn't a fig vine cover this side of the house?"

"Yes, but it died. Suddenly. Mysteriously. You won't believe what has died—the fuchsias from a blight, the hardenburgia from a freeze, and the fragrant rhododendrons after two El Niño winters in a row. I even lost holly and nandina, which are supposedly indestructible."

"What about the privet along the fence?"

"Oh, that was murder. First degree. I ripped them out to make way for clematis. But the worst loss was the beautiful white birch in back. That was the saddest."

Tomas's brow contorts in sorrow. He stares at me speechless. I realize I have delivered too much bad news too suddenly. He is a sensitive soul, still living in the past and parsimoniously, too, judging from his bygone Ivy League look: an old Shetland crewneck sweater worn over a white undershirt, boxy khakis, and frayed sneakers with white socks.

"But look, I don't kill everything!" I want to snatch him back from the jaws of death and thrust him into the warm, sunny present. "Changes are opportunities. I'd never have planted this dogwood to memorialize our last dog, Lizzie, if she and the holly tree hadn't died."

"It's beautiful," he concedes. "I see you still have the ivy...."

"Yes, and snails. After you objected, I stopped poisoning them. I went in for other forms of torture: tossing them across the street or suffocating them in plastic bags or letting them drown in beer or quickly crushing them underfoot. Lately, I've given up, but no matter how many I spare from now on, I know I'm destined to burn in snail hell."

Tomas looks pained. He holds his left elbow with his right hand and winces. I recall that he once spent time in a seminary. He probably takes my talk about hell literally. Anxious that I'm distressing him, I blunder on.

"After armillaria felled the birch, we planted lemon and

45

built a big deck. It's a real sun pocket, facing west. Let me show you."

Meeker proudly escorts us to the deck, his lookout post for squirrels.

"Your view is even more astounding without the birch."

"Here, have a seat. I'll get some iced tea."

I kick off my muddy clogs and go inside, barefoot. Through the kitchen windows I can see Tomas petting Meeker and talking to him, the kind of telling gesture that once made me melt. I used to look forward to Tomas's weekly visits with an excitement that seemed inappropriate for a married woman with two very young children. He'd arrive in his pickup truck with his handsome shepherd, Rolf, who never left his side. Tomas would croon to Rolf as he worked and often, between chores, would stop to stroke Rolf's magnificent ruff and rump. I knew then that if those strong, long-fingered hands ever traveled over my shoulders and flanks, I'd never leave his side either. I was afraid that the terrible force of my lust would grow too gigantic to conceal, and I became shy around Tomas. But now, simply glad to see him again, I feel relaxed and open. I regard him as a former lover, even though we had hardly ever touched.

We sit across from each other at the little round picnic table sipping iced tea and catching up. First, the safe preliminaries: the whereabouts of my children and husband, his little farm in Corvallis, the traffic congestion in the Bay Area. His sky blue eyes meet mine as steadily as ever. Gone are his sun-bleached ringlets, but his short clipped hair sets off his face like a silver frame. The kind wrinkles around his eyes and mouth and the sagging flesh of his neck assure me that our mortality is shared. His face looks thinner, his chin a bit longer. His left shoulder hangs lower than his right, his left hand rests motionless in his lap. Sometimes when he looks away, I detect a note of sadness, loneliness maybe.

"Whatever happened to Rolf?" I ask.

"He went with me to Oregon but died a couple of years later of lymphoma."

"Oh no. He was special, the real reason I hired you. You two had such a beautiful bond. Do you have a dog now?"

"No."

"Did you ever marry?"

"No," he says, smiling at me enigmatically. His lingering gaze could convey longing. It is accompanied by a blush, which I cannot interpret. I wish he had a dog. I don't want him to suffer.

"Do you live alone?"

"Yes."

Our talk continues with me interrogating him more than I want to. Perhaps he is deferring to me as lady of the house, or perhaps his nature is passive. I remember, though, that once he had guided me around the local nursery and was very much in charge in that setting. No, he tells me, he doesn't garden anymore, not since an arthritic condition afflicted his shoulder. Yes, the pain is pretty constant, but medication helps. Physical therapy hasn't done much.

"What about heat and massage?" I ask, imagining how well I could take care of him. He reminds me of the sad little boy my younger brother had been and of the fun we'd have when I cheered him out of his doldrums. Tomas shrugs skeptically.

With visions of becoming his healer, I press for the personal. Had he read the love story I'd written about him? It had appeared under a pseudonym in a local anthology. Yes, he had. Had it embarrassed him? A little. Was I way off the mark? No, not really. I wonder if our attraction was the reason why he had moved to Oregon, but I am afraid to ask. Rejection, even now, would sting. I sip the last of my iced tea and gaze at him over the rim of the glass. I think his face has grown more handsome than ever. The cheekbones seem more pronounced, the cleft in his chin a bit deeper....

"I was always dazzled by the level of your social activity," he says. "Carpooling all those kids, hauling groceries, cooking all that food. Do you still make those amazing oatmeal-chocolate chip cookies?"

"No, I forgot about those. Lately, it's ginger chip cookies and toffee. Want some?"

"Not now. This is perfect."

The sun has slipped behind a redwood tree leaving us in dappled shade. The heat from my gardening exertions has also dissipated, and I'm feeling cold. Tomas, in his sweater, claims to be fine.

"How's your shoulder?"

"It hurts. It always hurts."

"I have just the thing for you."

I go into the house to get my fleece pullover and return with a fluid-filled neck wrap that I have heated in the microwave.

"This stays warm for hours," I tell him as I drape it around his neck and shoulder.

"Mmmmmm."

Tomas leans back in his chair and closes his eyes. His face relaxes. "That helps."

I tell Tomas of the different kinds of bodywork I've been studying—the Alexander technique, Pilates, and yoga—and I offer him a hands-on treatment if he wants.

"Sure. Now?"

"If you're ready."

I note how easily I've extended my offer and how quickly he's accepted. Nothing this intimate could have happened twenty-five years ago. The voltage would have been too high, the conditions inappropriate, and the possible consequences too devastating. But now, trading the role of wanting-to-be-seduced for that of healer and crone, I purposefully assemble some props: a mat, a blanket, a rubber ball, a Dyna-Band, some books to use as lifts, and a flaxseed eye pillow.

After checking the range of movement and flexibility in Tomas's shoulder, we agree to do some passive alignment work to ease his pain and stiffness. I ask Tomas to lie down on his back with arms at his side, knees bent up, and feet flat on the mat that I have spread out at the sunny end of the deck. He obeys as unquestioningly as a schoolboy. Kneeling behind him, I slip a couple of books under his head to lengthen the curve of his neck. Then I slide my right hand under his right shoulder blade and hold it there while pressing gently with my left hand across his right collarbone. After five or six deep breaths, I can feel his shoulder relax and open. We repeat the exercise on his other side, the injured side, with encouraging results.

I become immersed in our tender work. A sequence of movements unfolds as if by some master plan, but really it is the plain result of my own years of practice. I have never applied my stockpiled knowledge to someone else before, and I am excited as much by the depth and span of my eclecticism as I am by the willingness of my student. I am so absorbed trying to tailor the movements to Tomas's needs that neither the warmth of his skin, the sweet smell of his castille soap, nor the gentle tug of his gaze can distract me. My hands want to give and give. I concentrate on the relief I want him to feel. I will it to pass through my thoughts and fingers straight into the heart of his deepest aches. I want him to feel light and floaty, as free of tension as a sleeping babe. "Breathe in. Breathe out. Stretch deeper on the exhalation. In. Out. Two more, at your own pace."

My curious hands travel across his chest, smoothing the startled pectoral muscles, which become warm and pliant under my touch. I shift position, moving to his side to massage the ropy swell of shoulder and biceps. My delighting hands gain confidence as they progress slowly toward the elbow, first the uninjured side, then the other slightly atrophied one. Remembering the delicious sensation of my own body opening to caring touch, I spend longer on this shoulder, wishing I could rejuvenate it with touch alone. I can feel his surrender and the map of his bones. His moans and sighs make me smile.

I lose track of time until the dog ambles over and collapses with a grunt alongside Tomas. Meeker rolls onto his back, exposing his underbelly to the sun. Ah, yes, I agree, it's time for *shavasana*, corpse pose. I place a blanket under Tomas's shoulders for comfort. I lift his feet and sway them slightly before setting them down. I turn his palms toward the sky and press my hands open over his for a moment of greater extension. I know the touch will reverberate long after it is over. I cup his fine head in my hands and move it gently from side to side before placing it down. His eyelids are closed, the eyeballs unfluttering beneath the lids. I slowly release my hands, squeeze each earlobe, and, finally, with my thumb, to leave an indelible sensory memory, I apply a spot of pressure to the center of his forehead where the third eye resides. I stand up and watch Tomas and Meeker lying side by side in *shavasana*. Neither stirs. I tiptoe off to finish up in the garden.

When Tomas eventually comes to find me, I am in the upper garden covering the remaining pile of manure with a tarp. He takes my hands in his, pauses, and says a simple thank-you. I look up into his sky blue eyes and think he looks taller, straighter. And then his arms are around me and he kisses me, there, in front of the house beside the picket fence at the end of the cul de sac. His kiss has conviction and more. It shows signs of genius as it gains momentum. One hand slips around the nape of my neck, the other presses the small of my back so that his pelvis and ribs emboss my torso, and his steely bulge dents my abdomen. And I don't pull away, not when my inner crone rises up in indignation and shrieks, "Don't let him do that!," not when my neighbor Christine drives past and turns her car around in the cul de sac. Not even when two skateboarders shoot by the fence and jump the curb to fly into the street.

II. Objects and Desire

Who has not felt the surge of pleasure in pursuing and finally winning a hotly desired object? More than once, we Ladies have fallen prey to material craving. The lure of a coveted thing can feel as palpable as physical seduction—and is so much less risky!

Our prized objects are undemanding and forever true. No matter what our age, the joy of possession can serve as a perennial springboard to passion. Here, in writing about attachment to certain material things, we have unwittingly revealed some secrets. Often in the stories that follow, the object of desire serves some devious need. For one Lady, the reappearance of a canceled check awakens the longing for a past lover. Another discovers in the purchase of an outrageous dress her unconscious wish to be noticed and wooed. From something as insignificant as a whiff of peanut butter to an item as portentous as a new house, our silent yearnings creep into the spotlight.

You are welcome to rummage through our treasured things. Though nothing special at first glance—an antique marble sink, an old mattress—they hold the keys to our telltale hearts.

Found Object

&% ELVIRA PEARSON

She walked into the bathroom, closed the door, and moved over to the fine old marble sink Will had procured for her under such heady circumstances many years ago. Actually, a plumber would describe it as a "lavvy." A "sink," for a tradesman, belongs only in a kitchen or laundry room. Lavvy or sink, she never looked at it without the day returning to her in crisp detail.

They had gone out for a drive in an effort to dispel feelings of irritation and boredom—with each other, with life— she didn't exactly know. Certainly friends would have described the marriage as a good one. It had lasted for three decades, and no one had reason to know that the intimacy they once shared had pretty much drained away. Nothing in particular had *happened,* and perhaps that was explanation enough for the emptiness she felt and had been feeling for longer than she could or wanted to recall.

They were driving on a back road just outside of Boston when they came upon what had obviously once been a stunning mansion. The roof was gone but many walls and cabinets and fixtures were still in place. A staircase careened its way into nowhere, a clawfoot tub stared emptily at the bluest of skies, and a massive stone fireplace glared coldly at the distant surrounding gardens, now filled with weeds. It looked like an oversized dollhouse waiting for a child to place the beds, the tables and chairs, the mama and papa and baby dolls that would make it seem a real home. That view was quickly supplanted by thoughts of French architect Corbusier who, believing that "a house is a machine for living in," exulted in exposing the heretofore hidden pipes and wires and other vital components that allow a building to function.

Dollhouse or avant-garde architecture, this half-demolished structure had excited her enough that she asked Will to stop. He parked the car off the road and they walked onto the property, wondering aloud to each other about what it had been in its day, this decaying ghost of a house. Will was clearly as intrigued as she. Dust swirled up around their feet as they walked and seemed to stick in their throats when they spoke. They prowled all around the building without noticing or being noticed by the two workmen out back. While Will walked around the downstairs area, she worked her way through the debris to the once-stunning circular stairway, now with posts missing or askew like fractured limbs, several of its steps broken through. She managed to reach the wide-open second story without mishap. Her eyes immediately went to the elegant marble wash bowl on its slender pedestal standing all by itself, bereft of walls and the privacy they once afforded.

She placed her open palm over its mottled surface and rubbed it lightly and tenderly, as if to warm its cool surface to life. Had a mirror been on the wall above it, she would have known that her eyes had widened and grown intensely bright, and she would have seen the flush that quickly spread across her face and down her neck. All she was aware of, however, was a white-hot desire to possess this object that she couldn't stop caressing. In a tiny corner of her mind, she knew that her lust for it was vastly out of proportion to its value or to her need: it was, after all, simply one more material object among so many material objects she had accumulated over the years of their marriage.

It was then that Will had caught up with her. He had started to admonish her for being so foolhardy as to mount the fragile stairway. "Don't you see how danger—" When he saw her face, he stopped mid-sentence. She turned to him, her hand still on the marble surface, and she knew from his expression that *he* knew, that he had seen her in this state before, that he immediately recognized the intensity of her longing. She was dimly aware from times past that it excited him to see her this way—that he might as well have come upon her dancing naked in the moonlight—and that he would, at this moment, give her anything she wanted. He put his hand on top of hers and smiled. "You want it, don't you?" he said, in a soft, husky voice she hadn't heard in a very long time. She answered him with a smile.

By the time they made their way back to the lower level, one of the workmen had walked in. Obviously startled, he was about to ask them just what the hell they thought they were doing, when Will interrupted him. His voice echoed through the open space where afternoon sunlight illuminated the floating dust particles that choked the air.

"Hello! Say, what are you doing with the fixtures up here?" he asked.

In the face of Will's direct question, the man seemed to forget whatever it was he had started to say to them, instead answering: "We'll just get rid of them. Take them to the dump probably. Nothing worth much here anymore. Place has been abandoned for years, you know."

He pulled a dirty handkerchief from his hip pocket and wiped the sweat and dust from his face.

"Do you suppose we could have that little lavvy in the upstairs bathroom?"

Will was obviously hoping that calling it "that little lavvy" would sufficiently diminish its value as an antique and its importance to them as an acquisition. It did seem a bit ludicrous to say "upstairs bathroom" but the man didn't seem to notice. He looked up at the exposed second-story rooms and said nothing for a long minute. Finally, he drawled slowly, "Well, I don't want you going up there—too danger-ous the way it is right now. I'd have to get it for you. But I don't know. I'm not really authorized to give anything away."

He turned back to face them, looking at them curiously, trying to size them up. Will reached for his wallet, pulled out a large bill, and handed it to him.

"I know it means taking you away from what you're doing, but we'd be much obliged."

She almost let a smile leak out when he said "obliged." When he had had a few drinks, Will sometimes did wonderful imitations of lines from old films—this one was right out of an early Henry Fonda western. As for her, she never knew how much money to offer in situations like this. In similar circumstances, she invariably suggested more than it took to make the deal. And never would she have had the gall to say

something like "we'd be much obliged," which fairly
screamed for a "ma'am" to close it out properly. At any rate,
whether it was the cash or the "obliged," the workman pock-
eted the bill quickly and called out to the other worker who
was nearby, ripping nails out of old boards. Clearly, something was being salvaged still.

"Say, Don. You think you could pull that little lavvy out
of the second-floor bathroom and haul it down here?"

Don got the message that he was under orders to do just
that. He mounted the rickety stairs confidently, seeming to
know exactly where to step, what to avoid, when to hold on
to the banister. The group of three stared up at him from
below, watching him pull a wrench from his weathered tool
belt and proceed to loosen the treasure from its rusty bear-
ings. After some small talk between Will and the demolition
supervisor, Don once again negotiated the precarious stairs,
carrying the pedestal under one arm, as a father might carry a
compliant toddler. Then he went back up to get the bowl.
She held her breath until man and bowl reached the bottom.

She and Will and Don walked together to the car. Will
opened the trunk and removed an old blanket, which the
men wrapped around the bowl and pedestal. Once the sink
was wrapped snugly and secured for the ride home, Will
closed the trunk and turned to Don, who stood resolutely in
front of him, neither moving nor speaking. Without a second's hesitation, Will reached into his wallet and handed the
man a ten-dollar bill. Don's expression hardly changed as he,
too, quickly slipped the bill into his shirt pocket, and, in
what seemed like the same instant, pulled out a cigarette,
allowing it to dangle, unlit, in his mouth. Will and Don

nodded at each other in what she regarded as the finale of one of those inexplicable male rituals, the same whether out here on an isolated parcel of land or in the boardrooms of Wall Street.

When they got back in the car, he put his hand on her knee, and they exchanged a look. His hand felt exquisitely warm. She was surprised at how her body responded to that simple touch. It was as if she were a teenager, she thought, sitting in the movies with a new boyfriend, both of them nervous and shy, wondering if or when he might reach for her hand—and oh, the thrill when he did. Silly, she told herself, as her mind drifted back to those days when a hand in a hand was enough to start bells ringing above, thunder roaring below. Once home, the gentle flirting continued. A passing look, a light kiss on her hair, a warm hand on her shoulder. The memory of how it once was, when he held her face in his hands, buried his own in her hair, touched her ever so softly as if she might otherwise break in two, overcame her. Struggling with a rush of sensations—of remembered love mixed up hopelessly with mounting desire—she wondered, fleetingly, why they had been so distant for so long. Consummation of these yearnings would wait, she knew; by nature as much as by age, they both took pleasure in the heightened feelings that came from delaying gratification.

Alone in the bathroom at last, readying herself for bed, she stared at her reflection in the mirror, something she had long since stopped doing. Watching her face succumb to time, especially while Will's creases and wrinkles simply added to his good looks, had called out every bit of grace-under-pressure she could summon. It was a story every

woman of a certain age knew well and struggled to let go of.
That appearances mattered at all—and they did—was something she deplored. On the other hand, bedded down in the
soft darkness, wrapping her legs around him, feeling his
warm hand move up her back and slip around to her breasts,
gasping softly at the hardness of him pressing against her
with an urgency she had all but forgotten, what matter how
either of them looked in the harsh glare of the day?

It was a glorious night, one she would not soon forget.
When they eventually extricated themselves from each other,
lascivious images of exposed interiors, deep, sensuous bowls,
and regal pedestals danced in and out of her consciousness as
she drifted off to sleep.

The Gold Dress

& ROSE SOLOMON

Only my mother knows how much I lust for Jeanne-Marc evening wear. Though I live like a peasant in Berkeley and never go anywhere glamorous, I do share her passion for flamboyant designs. Jeanne and Marc make the sort of finery you would need if a prince invited you to his coronation ball or to a banquet at his island villa. So when my mother phoned to announce that a liquidation sale was in progress, I dropped everything and drove straight to the San Francisco warehouse to buy whatever I could.

The scene was total devastation: tangled wire hangers hung from the clothes racks like skeletons left over after a feeding frenzy. A few over sized garments were flung over the crossbars. The only other customer poked through bolts of material that lay on a table, but nearly anything ready-to-wear was gone. I was too late.

Despondent, I checked out the makeshift dressing room. On a wall hook dangling from spaghetti straps hung a gold dress, an ankle-length sheath, shriveled, gutted, and forlorn. With almost no construction, it looked more like a nightgown than a dress. Not expecting it to do a thing for me but with no alternative, I took off my hiking boots, jeans, and sweater and slipped on the wisp of a dress.

The fabric, a permanently pleated polyester as light as silk, enfolded me like a warm kiss. It was not a harsh, brassy gold, but a soft champagne. I stood in front of the mirror, instantly aglow, even with my blue wool hiking socks on.

"That fits," announced the other customer, a large woman who by now was wedging herself into layers of left-over scraps. "Here, this jacket is too small for me." She wrestled her plump upper arms free and wriggled out. "You can have it. It goes with the dress."

I thanked her and took the crinkle-textured jacket, which instantly shrank back to its intended size. I tried it on tentatively. Form-fitting, with a deep V-neckline, it was not the sort of thing I would have chosen. A short zipper sporting a long, naughty tassel fastened in front, cinching me in and supplying its own womanly heft. The sleeves enveloped my bony arms and made me look as classy as a *Vogue* cover. And busty. Hourglass busty. Not me at all, but not an illusion either. I pinched myself to be sure. I was metallic. I was molten. I could be a diva or a film star! I could open in Las Vegas! If I didn't mind eclipsing my daughter, I could one day be the mother of the bride in this knockout ensemble. Without another thought, I bought the $800 jacket and gown for less than $89.

As I drove back home to Berkeley with the gold dress nestled at my side, my heart pounded with a crazy sense of possession. I owned a treasure that no one would suspect I had. Best of all, I had absolutely no use for it, which only heightened the profligate joy I took in keeping it. Behaving

so out of character made me giddy, and I suddenly realized
that I couldn't hang this last-of-a-kind gown next to the drab
untouchables that occupied my closet. It deserved nothing
less than a shrine of its own.

As if in a trance, I veered off the freeway and found a
shopping mall with a closet supply store. I bought the gold
dress a satin hanger, a cedar air freshener, and a sturdy, transparent garment bag all its own. Then I bought sweater and
shoe bags so that I could begin to segregate royalty from
hoi polloi.

I spent the rest of the day cleaning closets, mercilessly
discarding orphaned skirts, unironed blouses, and dusty,
warped pairs of shoes. I emptied a closet at the end of the
hall beside a full-length mirror and dedicated it exclusively to
Jeanne-Marc, past and present. I hung my modest collection
of five Jeanne-Marc creations in order of acquisition, like a
historical retrospective.

I waited until after dinner when my husband went to
work in his study before I unwrapped the gold dress from its
bag. I took it into the bedroom and tried it on with two pairs
of outdated evening shoes, a different shoe on each foot. I
hesitated before showing it off. My husband, Sam, hates
dressing up. We first met in jeans and have all our best times
in jeans. He cannot understand my infatuation with Jeanne-
Marc, and on the rare occasions when I wear such showy
costumes, he tolerates me with wary reserve. In those
moments I am not the person he thought he was marrying.
And he is right. In most things I take his feelings into consid-
eration, but when it comes to Jeanne-Marc, I don't.

With a heavy but unrepentant heart, I finally called from

the bedroom, "You'd better sit down. I have something to show you. You will laugh."

But as I waltzed self-consciously into his study, he didn't laugh. He just stared, surprised, and said, "Wow!" in a soft, awestruck way. I couldn't believe my ears and ran to the mirror to see once again for myself. "Yeah! Wow!" I thought.

"You'll need better shoes," was all he finally said.

So the next day I went shopping for shoes and found a pair on sale in exactly the same soft shade. They have a long tapered toe and a voluptuous curve in the heel, high enough to be snazzy but low enough to walk in.

That night after dinner, I put on my gold dress again, this time with the gold shoes. I felt unfamiliar even to myself, but the longer I wore the ensemble, the more comfortable I became. The polyester didn't wrinkle or resist. It was more supple and taut than my own aging skin. And the shoes felt lighter than feathers on my feet.

During the next few days, I kept getting up from my writing desk to steal to the closet to visit my dress. I'd unzip the garment bag and run my hands over the fabric with its seductive textures. If I'd been blind, I'd have chosen this dress. Its feel was almost alive, slightly warmer than room temperature, as if it generated its own heat. It awakened and altered my senses. I realized I was no longer craving chocolate or grilled chicken apple sausages sputtering with grease. I was no longer haunted by the fear that I was missing out on something. Life suddenly felt complete, and I could return to my writing with a heightened sense of purpose.

I never tried on the gold dress in the daytime, but saved it for after dinner, as a way of prolonging the pleasure. My nightly costume party required no companionship, though I liked having Sam in the next room doing his own projects. From the little telltale clinks and beeps, I knew exactly what he was up to—exchanging e-mails, tying flies, or gluing the rips in his tattered wet suit.

Each time I donned the gown, I busied myself with housework and allowed my imagination to soar. While mentally choreographing a torrid Cole Porter number with Gene Kelly, I organized Sam's closet to bring it up to a higher standard, a gold standard, so to speak. Then, still in my gold dress and dancing to "Ain't Misbehavin'" with Fred Astaire, I polished the medicine cabinet mirrors and the shower tile until our bathroom was fit for a queen.

"Wouldn't you like to go out in your new dress?" asked Sam from the bathroom doorway. "I think we should go to the opera."

I put the sponge down, disbelieving, and sat on the edge of the tub.

"What do you mean? We never go to the opera unless we're tourists someplace else."

He explained that his partner had gotten a walk-on role in *Carmen* and would parade as a matador for six seconds in a jeweled costume from Spain.

"It's the dream of a lifetime."

No sooner had I phoned for the best seats in the house, which cost much more than the gold dress, than our friend phoned to say that his scene had been cut. He would never get to be seen in his splendid costume and, as it turned out, neither would I. We ended up taking the subway in our street clothes because I could not bear to parade my gold dress past the curious stares of the homeless, the drunk, and the incontinent who frequent the sidewalks near the station.

The night after *Carmen*, filled with ideas for new choreography, I rendezvoused with my gold dress before washing the dinner dishes. I stomped a brisk flamenco around the bedroom and felt rich indeed, as if my secret gold stash, simply by being hoarded, had appreciated and accrued interest. It yielded a kind of emotional currency, a surfeit of happiness, that almost felt like generosity.

I twirled into the hall to get a better look in the full-length mirror. To my surprise Sam was already there, blocking my view. He was preening this way and that, admiring himself in a brand-new suit with price tags still attached— a short wet suit perfect for windsurfing in Hawaii or Baja. It was black and sleek with turquoise epaulets and a long zipper down the back. It made his long, white feet look cold and vulnerable.

"You'll need matching booties," I said, as laughter convulsed us.

We clasped each other in a spasmodic hug at seeing ourselves too truthfully revealed: a perfectly mismatched pair, playing out separate fantasies together in front of a floor-to-ceiling mirror.

"Come with me," Sam said as soon as our laughter subsided. "I know exactly where I want to take you in that gold dress."

He scooped me up in his arms and carried me to the bedroom.

"Yes, why didn't we think of this before?"

"You were always so busy cleaning," he said, setting me down gently on the bed.

His black neoprene and my gold polyester melded into a much overdue embrace. They meshed hungrily, amazing us with their supple stretch and eagerness for physical contact. Encased in such new and enthusiastic skins, we thrashed about like seals, one atop the other—slippery, wild things. His hot neoprene clung to my metallic dress with the force of suction cups. Rivulets of sweat dribbled down Sam's face and collected in the fold of flesh protruding from the tight collar. With one hand I reached behind his back, grabbed the tongue of the zipper, and slid it down all the way to his waist. With my other hand I peeled the wet suit off his shoulder and freed him from its simmering constraint.

"Thank you, thank you," moaned Sam.

"Now we know why it's called a wet suit."

It took both of us to wrestle it over his determined erection and down over his buttocks to get him free. By then, his suit was so entangled with my gold dress that they slid to the floor, knotted in an ecstatic climax.

Ménage à Trois

SABINA SEDGEWICK

They came before the morning mist had evaporated from our canyon. The growl of a construction truck heaving back and forth brought me to the window in time to watch the crane unfurl its neck toward the gigantic eucalyptus tree across the street.

The crane's thin head consists of pincers that politely clasp the giant's arm at the shoulder. Machine and plant look like two dinosaurs dancing in the mist. Out of the lacy foliage appears a man—a tiny, chainsaw-wielding Tarzan swinging on a rope—who amputates the arm. Secured between the pincers each limb is lowered into the monster mouth of a tree eater. Then Tarzan slices up the mighty trunk into bite-sized pieces, as if it were asparagus. The same fate awaits the eucalyptus's mate.

The pair of trees had towered side by side on the sloping wilderness for many years. They had even survived the fire that consumed this neighborhood in 1991. I'm filled with sadness and regret as I breathe in their pungent perfume. It lingers in the air for hours, the last farewell of once vibrant, mature giants turned to sawdust. All because my husband had persuaded our nice new neighbors from New York that eucalyptus trees have shallow roots and would crush our roof in the next big storm.

"Don't be silly," he said to me when I protested. "Eucalyptus are not natives. They've been imported by mistake. Their roots steal water from the oaks and redwoods that rightfully belong here."

As his imported German wife, I get nervous when he talks like that. These days I feel a certain solidarity with non-native plants, which are no longer tolerated in state parks.

I know my husband is not motivated by ecology. His sole concern is for the house.

My husband fell in love with her while I was visiting the grandchildren in New York. His was the first offer, made within hours after he walked through the rooms. He had never acted so impulsively, except when he asked me to marry him only two months after we'd met. His passion for this house was contagious even over the telephone. He faxed the offer. I signed and faxed it back. He never mentioned that our future home was in a natural disaster zone.

As soon as I got home, my husband gave me a quick tour. Once I saw the kitchen, his desire became my own. The realtors were already waiting on the patio like a wedding party for bride and groom. Happily, I added my name to the final contract, unaware that I had signed on for a ménage à trois.

I could see that our new house had sex appeal. Men notice this as soon as they step into the vestibule. Women are aware that they have been presented to a rival. Conversation stops or shifts to accolades as my husband leads our guests from room to room inviting them to pass their hands over the polished granite countertop, the silky texture of the plaster walls curving into arching passages, to insert their fingers into secret orifices and niches. "Feel how the copper railing fits into your palm," he sighs, then bounces up the spiral staircase, lit by a skylight at the top. "It's like going inside a seashell," says my husband, as the men ogle its cochlear shape. At the end of my husband's thrill-tours, the men congratulate him, "What a find! No wonder you moved."

The women are more reserved, "Don't you miss your cozy old house? All these big windows and white walls must be hard to keep clean."

What they really mean is that we had deserted our family home of thirty years like an aging spouse. I'd joke about changing houses instead of spouses. But now I know better. I know what it's like when the old wife stays on to oblige the young mistress. She's sent me on exhausting errands to shopping malls for a new set of wineglasses, only to make me return them because they don't fit her taste. She's made me throw out my wedding china, my heirlooms, my towels and sheets. She'll accept an expensive adornment from my husband—a new painting, commissioned for a special spot to bring out her colors, her moods—for a while.

She really prefers to be naked. She is a shameless exhibitionist. She wants lots of parties with lots of people milling around in adoration. Like a siren she lured me into the kitchen, filling my head with Martha Stewart fantasies. Guess who's cooking gargantuan meals on the six-burner stove and scrubbing the sandstone floors on hands and knees, sucking the dust from fossil cracks? For all I know the house may just be a disguise. Maybe some spirit woman is trying to insinuate herself into our marriage.

I could have dealt with a mistress in the house a lot better than with a mistress who is the house. My problem is not mentioned in any marital advice book I read. How could I complain about a situation that is unique and to whom? I thought of the feng shui book my husband keeps by his bed. It's about negative forces in the house. A student of his from Taipei gave it to him after inspecting the house for "chi" energy flow. Afterward, every memento from our trips disappeared from our shelves, along with the family photos, including our wedding picture, because clutter blocks the circulation of chi. Of course my husband's things are allowed to stay: his family's furniture, his books, his cardboard boxes full of unsorted papers, his old ties, and every shirt he's ever owned. This doesn't exactly turn me into a feng shui convert.

Still, I kept my feelings to myself until I saw an opportunity to illustrate my point.

We were attending an environmental dinner lecture about saving urban creeks. Our old friend Bob had brought the same guest as last month. I was not alone in finding her exhibitionistic behavior toward Bob distracting. Thanks to a recent mention in the business section of our paper, we all knew that she had an MBA from Stanford and was CEO of a Web software company. Instead of listening to the speaker—a personal friend of ours whose subject was the creek in front of our house—my attention was riveted on the pair. Bob's woman friend was practically sitting on his lap, caressing his back and then moving her arm up to his shoulders. I watched horrified as her arm wound around Bob's neck like a boa constrictor.

"Look at those two," I said to my husband, with a glass

of organic wine in my hand and a smile on my face. "That's what I mean about your obsession with the house. The house is draped around you so you can't pay attention to anything else." I kept my tone light, as if I were making a joke. "The house is your mistress."

"Why are you so worked up about Bob?" He was looking at me like Charles Boyer looked at Ingrid Bergman in *Gaslight.* I've compiled a forty-year registry of my husband's expressions, and *Gaslight* ranks at the top of my frustration-provocation scale.

"Surely the woman could restrain herself until they're in bed."

"Maybe not." My husband grinned. "Every old guy here would love to take Bob's place."

Bob was an important figure on the political scene. He had several ex-wives, children stretching over two generations, publications, and many friends, all competing for his attention. I realized that nowadays an MBA-CEO was just the latest model of trophy wife, who offered up their own achievements for trophy men like Bob.

So I tried to convince myself that in comparison, the house was nothing but a harmless midlife diversion for my husband to bridge the gap between his career and retirement. Instead of getting rid of the house, I thought, maybe I should try to convert my resentment into a positive energy flow—as feng shui taught.

To bring romance into forty years of married life, I enrolled us in a ballroom dancing class. To my surprise, my husband liked the tango and took to practicing the steps each day. My husband's idea of "practice" is to strive until he gets it right. I see nothing wrong with dancing just for fun, but in his eyes I was just fooling around because I couldn't synchronize my steps to his counting out loud.

Latin rhythms filled our house at seven in the morning, when our neighbors walked their dogs by our windows to see my husband dance—his arms reaching around an invisible partner, his back straight, his head high, his feet gliding across the floor. He'd forgotten I was there. He was dancing with *her*, pulled into her embrace by magnetic walls.

Our lessons were the prelude to a ball at the Fairmont Hotel. "We're not ready," declared my husband. "You didn't practice."

"You didn't want me to," I replied. This got me into one of those "you never" arguments that wives always lose. I cried. Husbands of our generation hate crying wives. We know this of course, but we can't stop, nor can we get therapeutic benefit from crying. I saw myself as Cinderella who never makes it to the ball and has to stay in the kitchen forever because her prince has fallen under the spell of an enchanted house. Instead of holding my tongue or switching my brain to the male channel, I again brought up his obsession with his house.

"You mean *our* house," he said reasonably. He had that *Gaslight* look. He was driving me mad.

        ॐ   ॐ   ॐ

When I came home from the grocery store this afternoon, something was definitely wrong. Sounds don't need to be loud to be heard all over the house. Somebody was groaning upstairs.

The door to our bedroom door stands wide open. I still recognize the grunting and breathing of strenuous lovemaking, but I can't imagine that it is my husband who is making these passionate exhalations. It's my husband. He is hovering over the floor, stark naked, his back glistening with perspiration, legs stretched out, and then crouched, his arms bend as he moves his buttocks up and down to the rhythm of hard sex. Jealousy sharpens my appreciation for his youthful tautness, his flexing thigh muscles, his tight buttocks, action flushed. I've always been attracted to this particular area of my husband's anatomy. As I'm watching him making love to the floor, I suddenly feel very possessive of his body and also of those languid, soft pine planks I had oiled and massaged with my own hands to bring out that special luster, showing off lighter amber veins between the sensuous darker shades of brown. I'm tempted to take off my clothes as well and to slide down under him. To feel my back on the smooth wood, to press my breasts against his sweaty ribs, stroking his lusty penis until it's ready to come home. Maybe this ménage à trois could work for both of us. How long has it been since we made love? And why have we been lying side by side in our custom-made bed like marble statues on top of a medieval tomb?

According to feng shui, bedroom mirrors reflect old emotions back while you sleep, and you wake up confused and insecure. But I'm awake and very aware that in the late afternoon sun streaming through the skylight, my rival looks golden and sleek and oh so young! Whoever she is, wherever her power is coming from, she's pushing me out of my husband's energy flow.

Leaving the grocery bags unpacked, I grab the keys to the RV and run. One look at the two eucalyptus stumps tells me my fate if I stick around too long.

The camper has been sitting faithfully in our parking lot for months. He seems to be wagging his tail like a neglected dog hoping to be taken for a walk. When I turn the ignition key, he pants and barks enthusiastically, and we are off.

Unlike the house, my husband and I had chosen the RV together, after years of searching and comparing every model with our leisure travel expectations. We'd brought him all the way from Iowa—exploring each clever convenience along with the commodious landscape opening up in front of our eyes. Broad-hipped rivers, soothing sycamores, and fastidious farms led us toward the Colorado mountains, mined raw. The splendid colors of the mineral remains made monumental paintings out of crumbling rocks. While we imagined what it must have been like to cross this hot, dry land by wagon train, our cozy camper provided us with ice-cold drinks and microwave cuisine. Until my husband became obsessed with our new house, Born Free (so named by his Iowa maker) was our magic carpet to the great outdoors. While I adjust the driver's seat to fit my legs, my old dream resurges: to drive across the continent from San Francisco to New York. "The time has come to be my own pioneer," I declare.

"Yes, ma'am," Born Free agrees as we merge onto I-80.

Born Free understands why I am spooked. After all, the house is our common rival. I tell him how she plays on my husband's fantasies. How she's quiet for his work, and surrounds him with music for his pleasure, his moods. How she shows off for his friends, and then exposes her erotic charm in solitude, just for him. "She's man-made, man-built, totally compatible with masculine desire."

Soon we are driving through the Sacramento Delta. On both sides of the road I see cornfields of such intense, glossy green I could be driving over a plastic tablecloth, with grain elevators rising into view like salt and pepper shakers meant for giant hands.

Although the landscape is familiar, it's not where I'm supposed to be. Instead of going east to New York City, I'm heading north to Yuba City—to Spring Lake, our favorite campground in May, when the Sierra foothills are still green and warm. We haven't been there for two years, not since the house usurped our weekend plans.

I had no idea that a fire had ravaged Spring Lake. Once a verdant grove of manzanita and oak, our usual campsite is now a jumble of gnarly, black branches and burned-out stumps. Raw devastation spreads from the hilltop to the lake. Iron barbecue grills stick up grimly beside metal tables, devoid of shade. The whole place looks like a parking lot. I must find another place to camp. But where?

At our old site, only the Jeffrey pines have survived. Their broccoli-green tops tease the glowing California sunset, tall enough to withstand the loss of lower limbs, unperturbed by the memory of a burning sky.

After two hours I still haven't moved. Lying outside on my yoga mat, I'm looking at the pines. Extending their graceful limbs from strong and straight trunks, they resemble multi-armed temple dancers with long fingernails. I am their sole audience. Nature has always pulled me out of turmoil and depression, but this time it has the opposite effect.

I question my own place on Earth. If I were a Jeffrey pine, I'd draw sap from deep roots grounded in nourishment, and channel it up to an ever-greening top. Yet, at sixty-five, I see no evidence of fresh growth in my life, no brand-new achievements to compete with the new house, which rose like a phoenix out the ashes of the 1991 Oakland Hills firestorm. I'm sure this resurrection attracts my husband to the house. Is that what got me scared? We had both agreed that it was time to sell the old brown-shingle bungalow, which every year nagged us for more repair, eventually a new foundation. So what went wrong? How could we have reached such a polar division, where he sees rebirth and I perceive the beginning of death?

The sound of a truck breaks into my somber contemplation. To my dismay, a thirty-five-foot motor home is pulling into the campsite next to me, polluting the air with diesel fumes and blocking my view of the Jeffrey pines.

I switch from contemplation to enemy watch. Who are they? How many are inside the monster-home? An elderly woman is directing the driver in the backing-up procedure into the narrow opening between two charred stumps. Flitting around the motor home's huge rear end, the size of a city bus, she looks tiny, elf-like. I hope the big rig won't fit into the slot. But it slides in and comes to rest.

The woman disappears inside. Now the driver emerges to plug in the power cord, attach the water hose, and roll out the teal-green awning. He's tall and thin; his jeans hang loose from his hips. His driving skills reveal a retired truck driver. He's a road-cowboy. He could be sixty or seventy, I really can't tell. He has that "don't mess with me" and "I can fix anything" assurance. After he's done with his tinkering, he brings out two camping chairs—top of the line, padded recliners-and sets them up beside a teal-colored table, with two tall plastic glasses. As a final touch to suburban decor, he fetches an extra pillow (teal leaves and yellow roses) for one of the chairs.

The road-cowboy opens the aluminum door for the little old lady, who holds onto his hand as she gracefully climbs down the aluminum stairs. Though she wears jeans, she could be stepping out of a carriage—the motor home's name is indeed Country Coach—and she allows him to adjust the chair with the extra pad for her.

Even when I go back inside my own RV, I look out the window to watch the pair. The old lady—probably my age— is listening with such rapture that I conclude she's hearing his stories for the very first time. From there I go on to deduct that they must be new to each other, which also explains his meticulous concern for her comfort. I am not surprised that they hold hands when they stroll down to the lake, reflecting the last rays of sun like a mirage. I never lose sight of them. Sometimes they stop to take turns observing the Canada geese through a pair of binoculars. She's obviously the expert naturalist. She bends down to point out things for him, a nest, I suppose, or herbs and flowers she looks up in her book. She does all the talking now. From the way he holds his head I gather that he listens with great interest.

"Just look at those two," I say as if my husband were next to me. "They are actually kissing."

I'm sure they are late-blooming lovers, or high school sweethearts who met again after many years. Maybe they almost had an affair long ago, but she felt too guilty to leave her husband. This reminds me that I should call my husband. I haven't turned the cell phone on at all. Even if I am running away, I should tell him where I am. But the signal keeps roaming without reaching home.

I don't sleep well. I've never camped out on my own. I search in vain for my collection of maps and AAA travel guides. For years I've been holding on to boxes of maps and travel information for this trip across the continent, but in my hurry to leave I didn't even think of bringing them. All I find is a copy of the feng shui book, underlined by my husband. So I read that instead and hear us discussing it, as we do with many books.

I get up at dawn. Surveying once more the wreckage from the fire, I discover more and more signs of survival: in the soft morning light appear pennyroyal, Chinese houses, harlequin lupine I've never seen before. They'd never had a chance to grow in the dense brush, cleared now by the fire. And so is Spring Lake, shimmering in full view under a thin veil of mist.

What fascinates me is the contest for space between new and surviving plants. After decades of human control, nature is beginning to reestablish harmony by balancing the yin force of fire with the yang of rock and earth. In the soothing morning light the burned remnants of tree trunks glisten like oriental lacquer vases, arranged among delicate grasses in shades of gold, brown, and gray. A closer look at a dead manzanita tree reveals a sprig of green at the tip of a parched branch. A monarch butterfly has already settled on the pendant of tiny pearl flowers. I take comfort in the thought that growth coexists with seeming chaos and decay. According to the basic principles of feng shui, yin and yang form a circle in which one moves toward the other from polar opposition to subtle blending; one side becomes the other. Perhaps I could learn something here about my own transition to the next stage after middle age. Maybe my husband and I share the same circle, both running toward the end, both looking for renewal, forever trying to catch up, without recognizing that yin and yang must blend and balance?

When I return to my RV, my neighbors are already eating their breakfast under the teal awning. They give me a friendly wave. I respond with a smile. But I don't stop by. I don't want to intrude on their togetherness. I prefer to study the pair as human wildlife in their camper habitat. From my perspective, they are in fact an endangered species: an elderly couple in love.

When I look out my window in order to resume my observation, I can't believe what I see: my husband's Camry is parked in the shade of the Jeffrey pines. My happiness surprises me.

In the camper, he says exactly what I expect: "Are you ready to come home now? You have no idea how worried I was. I stayed up all night waiting for you to call. When I saw the RV gone, I thought maybe you'd driven up here. What's gotten into you all of a sudden?"

"I'm going back to Iowa, and then all the way east to New York. You know, just as we said we would after we bought Born Free."

"All by yourself? What about me? We were going to make the trip together!"

"You have the house to keep you company."

"It's too lonely without you there. I've missed you."

I smile. I pull down the shade and put my arms around my husband's neck. "Kiss me."

He pecks my cheek.

"On the mouth."

He brushes my lips.

"No, *really* kiss," I say.

And he does.

Sweet and Hot: A Recipe

✑ CLAUDIA MORTON

Sweet and hot are wonderful qualities in men and in culinary creations. I am acquainted with a chef of genius who was not too happy in his native France and is often not too happy in California. He is highly trained and creative but not interested in the fast track of big city restaurants; he is both of the world but at odds with it. If he seems distant, it may be that he is thinking about his chess game.

He is handsome and slender because he does not consume more than a sampling of his creations. This is a mystery to me, because I find them almost addictive. Here is his recipe for Sweet and Hot Jalapeño Jelly, which, he says, is not really his, having come to him from an unremembered source:

> Take three bell peppers—one red, one green, one yellow—and three jalapeño peppers. Rinse, seed, and dice them finely. If you like, dice some fresh ginger and combine it with the peppers. Put six cups of sugar in a pan and slowly blend in one and a half cups of apple cider and the diced peppers. Heat while stirring until it reaches a hard boil for five minutes. Now add twelve ounces of pectin, still stirring, and bring back to a boil for exactly one minute.

Cool slightly and transfer to heated jars as you would any jelly and seal before setting aside to cool.

Put a good tablespoonful of this condiment on the plate with any mild-flavored meat—turkey, chicken, veal sausage with red cabbage—and it suddenly comes to life.

Jalapeño jelly holds its own with more flavorful meats as well, like duck or wild game. With roast lamb, it can replace mint jelly or mint sauce. Ham accommodates it happily in place of the traditional pineapple or sautéed fruit, and roast pork pairs with it in place of applesauce.

Try this jelly and you'll never want to be without it. It is with good reason that we look to the French for sensual guidance. Start with dinner and go from there!

Government Issue

☃ BERNADETTE VAUGHAN

Did the peanut butter come to England first, or did they? Both epiphanies were abrupt and mysterious. In the dreadful, dispassionate, impeccably articulated BBC bulletins—always preceded, for the nightly nine o'clock news, by the sound of Big Ben: *bong, bong, bong, bong, bong, bong, bong, bong, bong*—I never heard anyone say that today, or tomorrow, or perhaps next week, they would arrive. Neither did I hear any mention on the morning and midday news, communiqués announced by three staccato and rather lighthearted pips that made me suspect that God's attention to the gravity of the situation might be wandering. But the subject of the two impending arrivals must have been discussed. Or perhaps not: there was A War On, after all, and in my seven-year-old view anything could happen.

The War saturated the fabric of existence. It was a way of life, an austere discipline taught sometimes by firsthand experience and the rest of the time by radio broadcasts. Both smoked and branded the spirit, raising keloid-like lesions that, more than half a century later, make me wonder if, after so many centuries of played-out bloodlust fantasy, the world's soul has grown into one huge, nerveless, rubbery lump. Every day, I listened carefully to the news. The information was always devastating, always conjuring images that made me want to run screaming in search of a place of safety. Somehow, though, the measured monotones that delivered it brought something predictable, oddly soothing, into my exploding perception of the world.

"This is the BBC Home Service. Here is the news and this is Alvar Liddell reading it. Bombs fell at random. The Enemy suffered heavy losses. The Allies suffered heavy losses. Some of our aircraft are missing. The next of kin have been informed."

On none of the BBC newscasts did I hear anything about the approach of either peanut butter or the Americans.

Peanut butter arrived one day, at school, at Hall Assembly, the convent's ritual quotidian gathering of teachers and pupils for prayers, announcements, and exhortations. We marched in, form by form, kindergarten first, upper sixth last, as always to the strains of the brisk martial music that Miss Jones, our gym teacher, chose as an antidote to the languorous, pheromonal waves oozing from our burgeoning womanhood. And there, behind the headmistress Sister Genevieve, waiting in all her billowing blackness to discipline and direct our day, was the peanut butter, undisclosed in what looked like stacked petrol cans. None of us paid much attention to it; there was always something up there on the stage, some scenery being constructed or refectory table mended or schoolroom desk in the process of refurbishment. The relentless femininity of the convent allowed for no workshop. God alone knew what virile possibilities such a facility might conjure: stripped torsos, dripping sweat, gleaming muscles, matted body hair. Holy Mother preserve us! A far cry indeed from the pale clerics in floor-length black *soutanes* who heard our confessions.

So the large open space of the stage was utilized by two grizzled and taciturn odd-job men the nuns employed for purposes of convent structural upkeep. For major projects they would bring in reinforcements: prisoners of war, hapless German airmen plucked from trees and marshes like trapped and wingless raptors, disentangled from their collapsed parachutes by an elderly and irate Home Guard given to querulous commands and surreptitious prodding with the business end of an obsolete firearm.

All of us at the convent, nuns and pupils alike, were thrilled by the prisoners. *Frissons* of alarm and delight rippled our flesh when we encountered them in the orchard on our way to the hockey field. We conjectured in low voices that perhaps they were spies, heroically intercepted before they could send the signal, who knew what it was—the flashing light, the nightjar's rattle—that would flood England with invading enemy hordes, looting, pillaging, despoiling; but, we reassured each other and ourselves, now that they were among us, now that they knew us, knew how kind, how understanding we were, they would not dream of doing any of these dastardly things. We were grateful for that and very polite, very kind, to the haggard young men; we younger pupils, not yet awakened, viewed them with curiosity and awe and demure flirtatiousness. Our imaginations ran riot among them, particularly when those prisoners who held religious convictions joined us in prayers at Hall Assembly. They stood silently to the side, thin, remote, their blond heads bowed, their eyes occasionally flickering in the direction of the buxom Upper School girls. The upper fifth and sixth forms were allowed to discard, in favor of gored skirts, the wool serge gym tunics that were the official uniform for the Lower School; the Bold Girls, already identified and carefully monitored for provocative behavior—giggling, poking each other, Making Spectacles of Themselves—by sharp-tongued nuns, wore eye-popping wool sweaters and belts cinched tight.

That day, the peanut butter day, we marched in and fervently recited all the prayers, especially the one for the conversion of Russia, which daily reminded me that I was not the stuff of which martyrs are made since I knew I would render unto the Communists my craven soul without a second's thought if one of them so much as mentioned the instruments of torture. As we recited the belligerent words (*Holy Michael, Archangel, defend us in the day of battle, Be our safeguard against the wickedness and snares of the Devil; May God rebuke him, we humbly pray, and do thou, Prince of the Heavenly Hosts, by the power of God, thrust down to Hell Satan and all wicked spirits who wander through the world for the ruin of souls),* I wondered again why we never prayed for the conversion of Hitler, because, given the preoccupations of the period, you would have thought that would be a much more urgent and appropriate jogging of the Almighty's elbow. Perhaps, I mused, there was some arcane article of war that expressly forbade such intercession, perhaps because it would have been rude to the already subdued prisoners for us to do so, out loud and with everybody looking, as it were. We prayed, as always, that we might remain pure in thought, word, and deed. We prayed for our gallant soldiers, sailors, and airmen, those alive and facing danger for us and those who had already lost their lives. Then we sang the hymns, usually featuring the one that went *Faith of our fathers, living still / in spite of dungeon, fire, and sword* that I particularly hated because it seemed to describe the experience of being in an air-raid shelter with fiery death raining down outside and invading German soldiers—not our sad-faced prisoners, but real, glint-eyed, rasping soldiers, with helmets and hand grenades and bayonets—waiting to blow me to smithereens or run me through when I emerged, hands held high, no matter how ardently I pleaded for my life. After the hymns, which signaled the completion of our devotions, Sister Genevieve cleared her throat and announced that Reverend Mother was on her way from The Other House— where the nuns lived and where the Parlour was, beyond the orchard and across the cropped lawn that vanished under an enormous, drooping cedar of Lebanon—to speak to us.

This was portentous news.

Reverend Mother Superior was an ancient, diminutive Frenchwoman who spoke very little English. She was rarely sighted. On her Feast Day, she would emerge cautiously from The Other House and appear at Assembly, where the choir would sing *J'irai revoir ma Normandie / C'est le pays qui m'a donné le jour* because she was from the north of France and missed her home. Then the Head Girl, in her second year of sixth form before university, would make a demure speech in French, then curtsy and present one of the "babies" from the convent nursery school, who, lower lip quivering ominously, would grumpily hand over the gift to which we had all under pressure contributed our pocket money. Then Reverend Mother would weep and, first unfolding an enormous handkerchief that looked like a quartered bedsheet, blow her nose as if it were Gabriel's trumpet and murmur in her papery old voice, *"Que Dieu vous benisse, mes chers enfants, que Dieu vous benisse."*

That day Reverend Mother emerged from the wings onto the stage, smiling nervously as we chorused, *Bonjour, chère mere!* and the more adventurous among us tried to remember what they might have done, if they had been seen abroad without their gloves, or in the company of boys from Presentation College on the other side of town, or, much worse, *in their hair,* which is to say, without the uniform velour with the distinctive brown and gold St. Joseph's hatband. This last was a crime equal to treason, lewdness, or punching the pope. (I carefully sewed a piece of elastic to mine in a tight U-shape, to anchor it under my chin in case of a wayward gust of wind.) Sometimes, when there was a crisis that might involve someone's expulsion, Reverend Mother was hauled out of seclusion to witness, with much emotion, the sentencing. I was feeling particularly vulnerable that day because, the day before, while running on the way to the chapel, I had tripped over the pedestal of the statue of St. Michael serenely impaling the Prince of Darkness, in vanquished dragon form, on his spear. I landed, on my back with my gym tunic over my head and all my underwear exposed, right at the feet of Reverend Mother, Sister Genevieve, and Mark Henry, Lord Bishop of the Diocese, who was visiting.

"Ah, Glory be to God," said Sister Genevieve, her mouth a thin line of suppressed fury as she hauled me to my feet. She had a grip like the Commendatore. Scarlet with mortification and close to tears, I glanced at Reverend Mother and Mark Henry, noting that their mouths were each frozen in a silent O of amputated speech. "Tis a bold girl y'are. There'll be a black mark on yer report at term's end for ye to explain to yer parents, see if there isn't. Now kiss His Lordship's ring and take yourself off. Begone."

Today, however, there was no talk of expulsion nor of black marks of any kind. Today, Sister Genevieve explained, with Reverend Mother standing by, she would bestow the transatlantic gift of peanut butter, which America had sent to help us in our darkest hour. Now we would all understand why we had been asked, during the preceding two weeks, to bring to school from our mothers' kitchens the tall bottling jars that were among the emblems of female patriotism at the time. No housewife fit for the title let a season pass without conserving its bounty in her bottling jars against a looming period of even greater deprivation. Even eggs got bottled.

"*C'est vraiment gentil de leur part*," said Reverend Mother apprehensively, as we trooped up on stage and one by one took delivery, via Sister Genevieve's angry spatula, of our allotted portion of an ambiguous, mustard-colored substance. "*Ils sont très sympathiques, ces Americains. Il faut les remercier. Et de toute façon...*" she paused for a moment, eyeing the oily mass that that plopped sullenly from the spatula and oozed along the bottom of the jar, "*...ça doit être vraiment, que dirais-je, pratique, hein?*"

Nobody mentioned that this was a gift of food.

"It's for our shoes," I said to my sister when I saw her in the playground later. "For the leather. You rub it in, to make it waterproof."

It seemed to me that if the Americans knew nothing else about England, they must know that it rained a great deal here. The weather, after all, was the main topic of conversation among strangers.

"*No!*" said my sister, scornfully telegraphing her dreaded really-little-sisters-are-the-absolute-limit censure. "It's for our *hair*, silly." She applied a cautious dab to the end of one of her plaits. "To make it shiny. See?" I inspected the sticky strand. It was shiny all right. "All Americans have very shiny hair," she explained more kindly. "It's not just the film stars."

She knew this because we went to the movies (we called them "the pictures") every Saturday and film stars did indeed have very shiny hair. Ordinarily, I would have taken her word as gospel, because I was the youngest, but I was skeptical about this particular assertion because English film stars had very shiny hair, too, and this, this—whatever it was in the jars we were holding—simply did not feature in any of the English film magazines that we brought into the house.

By the end of the day I had learned from close observation of my peers that peanut butter was meant to be eaten. It was for people, not for more recognizable peanut ingesters like the elephants and monkeys at Regent's Park Zoo. The Americans ate it all the time, apparently; now they were sharing it with us because the stringent rationing that prompted my parents to grow vegetables and keep a flock of messy, excitable chickens was a cause of loving concern to them. Far away, and preoccupied as they must be living the luxurious, optimistic, musical lives we saw depicted in the movies, the Americans cared about us. And, dubiously studying the contents of my glass jar, I concluded that I cared about them in return. Thus do food and love become inextricably entwined.

The Americans arrived out of nowhere, one day in the summer of 1942. Suddenly, they were everywhere. Tall and glamorous, their amazing white teeth gleaming in puzzled, hopeful smiles as, aghast and overwhelmed with excitement and terror, they struggled to come to terms with their collective status as heroes and wondered how—when they got home, if they got home—they would tell the tale of their adventures on this tiny, truculent, fog-bound island. Soon they were traipsing shyly up the damp path, bordered by rhododen-drons, that led to the front door of our house, thrown open by my mother as part of her war effort, for Friday supper, for Sunday lunch, for noisy, jitterbugging weekend parties. Homesick, appalled by the meagerness of English rations and dumbfounded by the drabness of English life, the young soldiers and airmen brought gifts of silk stockings and great slabs of steak. Desperate to be perceived as civilized in that historically rich and brutally stratified culture, they added chocolate and thick, satiny magazines. Uniformed or civilian, English males hated them. *They're overpaid, overfed, oversexed and over here.*" The refrain was groused in every pub across the land as English females— ordinarily circumspect but suddenly weary of pinched expectations—bundled patriotism and other virtues into a single threadbare bundle, tossed it to the winds, and succumbed to enchantment, impregnation, and ultimately, for some, expatriation.

I loved them. They were beautiful, affectionate, and kind. They wore crisp, pinkish beige and green uniforms; they picked me up and swung me high over their heads; they called me and my sisters and even my mother "honey." I made no distinction between the officers we entertained and the enlisted men who waited somberly outside in the village street, jackets unbuttoned, their cigarettes pinpoints of red light in the summer dusk as they guarded the Jeeps in which they would ferry their superiors back to barracks. Sometimes, bearing in mind my mother's dictum that you never leave a guest unattended, I would leave the house to take cake or lemonade or other refreshment to the startled drivers. I did not want them to be bored as they waited. I climbed into the passenger seat and engaged them in decorous, animated conversation about their homes, their backgrounds, their schooling; I volunteered information about my parents, my siblings, my friends. When, inevitably, they offered handfuls of chewing gum, I primly refused it, finding this gesture of ingratiation (officially sanctioned by Allied High Command to sweeten the more tart edges of culture shock) offensive. *I* was the hostess, the welcomer; *I* was the dispenser of grace and reassurance and largesse. I was not to be mistaken for a pitiful mendicant, certainly not to be confused with the shameless local louts who jeered and yelled, *"Got any gum, chum?"* and sniggered at the standard response: *"You got a sister, mister?"*

I loved the magazines they brought, though; I learned a lot about America from them, in those days before the American War of Independence and the orange groves of California became an essential part of my Upper School studies. The magazines, extravagant and overwrought, pulsed with information about the rites of passage entered by adolescents in open cars under harvest moons and instructions on how to avoid giving offense with body odor. Such odor, I noticed, was given a lot of space in the magazines, where it was portrayed as a rampant, though veiled, social sin. At school, Miss Jones, reprovingly throwing open the gymnasium windows, would say: "It's stuffy in here, girls!" and we all knew what she meant. When I read the phrase "giving offense," I felt a flood of dark guilt. I always suspected that I was the reason for the stuffiness, but now the magazines hinted far more darkly, much closer to a more scary edge of possibility. In the American magazines, women were always the perpetrators of the offense, men were the outraged victims. It all had to do with being married. In one comic strip-style advertisement, a perturbed husband stared in accusation and slow-dawning disgust at his wife, who, dazed and distraught, covered her mouth with one hand and with the other tried to ward off the unspeakable specter of rejection invoked by her spouse's indignation. "He's said he's leaving! But I bathe every day!" Thus in the next picture the weeping wife to a female friend, who looked concerned but relentless and stern. Plainly, the next step would be the husband's decampment. And serve her right. Who was she, this despicable giver of offense, to expect succor from her friends? Dismayed, I concluded that the advertisements were cautionary tales; if I understood them correctly, women who gave offense in this mysterious, unnamed but *married* area— and what did it mean? *What did it mean?*—were abandoned. American men simply packed up and left.

This was horrifying to me. I did not understand that the advertisements reflected a peculiar national preoccupation, at its most ardent during the '40s and '50s among Americans: they were selling douches. I would have been doubly per-plexed if I had understood. Raised in a household where French and English were interchangeable, often startingly so, and frequently occupied the same sentence *("Chérie, rape for me the cheese, s'il te plait")* to me a douche was a shower and wartime austerity rules forbade such luxury. I simply knew that the gorgeous, beloved Americans, our saviors, were actually *here*, in England, my world, where hot bath water was rationed to five inches a week per person. What would happen if they became overwhelmed by all the offense that I was sure by now the English, unread, unwashed, and unwarned, were giving? Would they just leave, like the hus-bands in the magazines? The thought made me grope around in panic because now I loved the Americans with a profound, adhesive yearning; I could not bear to lose them.

Worriedly turning the glossy pages of the magazines for some clue as to how best to appease my potentially aggrieved love objects, I came upon opulent pictures of food so florid, so extravagant, that, clearly, the chances of my being equipped to beguile our guests into forgiveness by reproducing it were nonexistent. How in the world could I conjure, even given the prolific rhubarb that flourished in my parents' kitchen garden, the baroque assemblage of a molded Jell-O salad? And no less mystifying than peanut butter, although, since Sister Genevieve's distribution, alto-gether more remote, were the desserts, garlanded with glamorous names—*Shoefly Pie, Icebox Cookies, Apple Pan Dowdy*—that I discovered in the advertisements. But the really compelling ones, the ones captioned with words that rumbled like faint thunder—*Angel Food, Devil's Food*—came out of boxes.

Years later, in the '60s, freshly arrived in the States and struggling to incorporate superabundance, conspicuous consumption, and planned obsolescence into my perceptions of the new found land, I gasped in recognition at the pictures on the Betty Crocker cake mixes I saw on a supermarket shelf. Stopped in my tracks, yanked into the jungly depths of twenty-year memory, I was mugged by the unforgettable, unforgotten image of a huge, uniformed, crewcut Texan: Mickey O'Brien, best beloved of all the American soldier/airmen, who smiled like the sun, who leaned from his cathedral height and said I was sure pretty. I was his sweetheart, he said, and he would take me with him, back to America, when the war was over and he returned from France. And now here I was a grown woman and shortly to be a mother and I swept the boxes from the supermarket shelf and, time executing flawless backward somersaults at my heels, ran for the exit. I almost forgot to stop at the checkout. All I wanted was to dive into the evanescent past and see his face again, dance with him again, handsome, laughing Mickey, Archangel and defender, my once and forever love. And I remember now how frantically, back at the house, I stirred the cake mixes and poured the batter into baking pans and how bitterly I wept when I pulled the results, one black, one white, from the oven and bit into them. Because, dear God, Angel and Devil were equally, abysmally dreadful; pictured on the box, they made the past reel with sickening vertigo; manifested, they tasted like the secondhand air that gets trapped in the soles of old sneakers.

But back in my childhood, in that suspended, embroidered time before D-Day, poring over the lustrous magazines, the names of these products, *Angel, Devil*, only proved what I suspected: that our lucent deliverers must themselves be divine emissaries, sent by God, tall and tanned in their warrior colors of mushroom and fern, moving among us with music and marvelous, loose-limbed dances, speaking peppermint words with tongues of flame.

"*Mairzedotes*," they sang. "*Un dozeydotes un liddlelamm-zeedivy, a kidderleedivytoo wooden yoo?*"

"*Onda achesontopeka anda sannafay.*"

"*Chattanoogachoochoo, wontchachoochoomee home?*"

Dispersed by the airwaves, these anthems riveted together the scaffolding of my being. Salvation and damnation wrestled between the lines of the songs and the comic strip advertisements; in the pictures of celestial or infernal cakes; of repentant wives and departing husbands; of ardent, blameless teenagers in their open cars; and in the emblem that I loved best of all: Ivory soap, so pure, so untouched by base human shortcomings that its logo took the stately and sublime shape of a swan. Here was the central and transformative core of cleanliness, of salvation: a substance that walked on water, unsinkable, denying to the depths their dominion. To use it was to waft toward God, to be pleasing unto His nostrils at last: Ivory the swan, sent with the Americans as a sign of His receding wrath in the dark dragon days, a promise of hope that everything would be all right in the end.

I would try to remember this as I listened to the news of the D-Day landings and, numb with an adult and searing grief, overheard the grown-ups talk about the bravery and death of Lieut. Col. Mickey O'Brien in Normandy. Or, later, as I watched newsreel pictures of the young Americans riding their tanks into battle, or fanning through the fields, scaling the hedgerows and earthworks with bayonets fixed, grimy-faced and exhausted under their steel helmets. Or wafting on parachutes, misty-white, fluorescent, souls released and transformed and flying away, back to America, back home, far from the war that caught them, at last, on barbed wire and strung them, like swans, on lines of tracer bullets. Life everlasting in songs, perhaps, in shiny photographs and Technicolor layout, but not here, not here in England, in Europe, in fire and loss amid the bleakness and the terror of war.

Sometimes, late at night, if I can't sleep, I go to the kitchen and take the peanut butter—a robust staple of my American husband's diet—from the refrigerator. I scoop some out with my fingers and put it in my mouth, let it rest on my tongue, spread over my palate, and slide down my throat. It is still, after all this time, alien and mysterious; lately it has become slightly laughable, flaunting its salted or unsalted, creamy or crunchy pretensions before the *haute* discriminating stare of *cuisine.* But I salute its generosity, its pragmatic and sturdy resilience, and standing there in my nightgown in the shadowy kitchen, bathed in chilly white refrigerated light, I consider rubbing my oily fingers through my hair and on the leather soles of my slippers....

And I settle for wry thanks, for survival, for the reminder that love and war are not necessarily coupled, for finding in this humble, enduring, heroic substance my consolation on dark nights.

Checks and Imbalances

✀ ELVIRA PEARSON

The check you write in pleasure, you cash in pain.
—Italian proverb

Check #1104 dated August 1, 1975, kept surfacing years after Dan and I had broken up and my heart was no longer strewn about in a million pieces. I had moved many times since then, and that check, made out to Dan Friedman, had moved right along with me. I had no explanation for why, in the first place, I had impulsively pulled #1104 out of its proper numerical home between #1103 and #1105 and put it aside. In the weeks and months after one of my many moves, the day invariably came when I would open up a box and there it would be. The experience of finding the check was always the same: I was never looking for it, it seemed to drift mysteriously into my waiting hand, and he was never on my mind when it happened.

I had written the check on our trip to Mexico, a trip we took—at my foolish suggestion—to erase the memories of our last disastrous trip: Dan, in the heat of his passion for me, wanted to show me the Europe he knew, but we returned home barely speaking. "Let's put this behind us and do it

99

again," I had said in one of the ubiquitous fluorescent-lit airport cafeterias where we stopped after debarking from Paris.

That Mexico City trip in many ways was more agonizing than our trip to Europe, my first and only visit to Paris, Rome, Venice, Florence. In Europe, we were still giddy in love and managed to use fitful lovemaking to dispel angry, hurt feelings that gathered momentum as the weeks went by. In Mexico, Dan rolled over in bed at the end of the day and turned to stone.

I suppose there was something elusive we each wanted from the other. Whatever it was, neither spoke about it. On our first morning in Paris, I was as shocked at his barking angrily at the concierge when she knocked on the door with our croissants and coffee as he was dismayed that I didn't want to tramp through Europe for hours *au pied,* see every historical edifice Paris and Italy had to offer, and walk through room after room after room of museums. He did not squirm as I did at claustrophobically small elevators that moved us up floor after floor like the proverbial molasses going uphill in January until, mercifully, we reached a landing where I could open the screeching accordion door and bolt out. He was what is referred to—now I know—as a "seasoned traveler." I could not have been greener.

Each day in Europe, I vowed to try harder to make this trip work. After all, we were grown adults, each of us with children from a previous marriage. But every day brought a new misery. As hard as I tried, by dinnertime, we were often not talking. In utter frustration one evening on our way to dinner (he had just told me that the dress I was wearing made me look pregnant), I pleaded with him to tell me what I could do to make things better. He paused a second and then said, "Just don't be so mad at me."

After we got home, his friends at work reassured him that travel can break up even long-standing marriages. It was obvious that we hadn't taken this veiled advice seriously, because we had no sooner landed in Mexico City than it all started happening again, beginning with my disbelief the very first night that he didn't object to the twin bed arrangement in the hotel room. The thought occurred to me that he might have even *requested* twin beds. I had to push that idea down; it was too unbearable. For the next several nights, I remember lying in the crevice between the two beds (naturally, I had pushed them together) curling myself around his stiff, unwelcoming back, refusing to hear the message he was delivering.

On one of the brighter days of that trip, we strolled around the city window-shopping. I spotted a perfect little rug at a perfect little price. I hadn't brought any money with me, so I asked Dan to pay for it. I'd write him a check when we got back to the hotel. In the interval between my writing the check and the bank returning it with my statement, it had taken on its special, painful meaning. Except for those occasions when the check jumped into my hand, I saw the pain of those trips and our eventual breakup as being safely locked in the past. Surely, one would think, the many intervening years and new relationships had smoothed over my feelings of hurt and betrayal.

Not so. The day came when I was rummaging through my white cardboard filing boxes in search of a document I needed. In the third box, there it was, on top, casual—

impudent almost—taunting me to pick it up and go through the ritual of staring at my handwriting and then turning it over to stare at his scrawled endorsement on the back. Knowing what I had not let myself know before—that the grief from those days was simply dormant—I succumbed to the memories that tumbled out.

We had a lovely beginning. We had met at a house party given by a friend. I remember wearing an elegant copper-colored satin dress and dancing up a storm all by myself, well aware that his eyes were on me. We flirted our way through the evening, talked some and laughed a lot, and he finally asked me out. When I tried to explain that I was in but about to get out of a relationship—Giorgio had gone home to Italy for the Christmas vacation—Dan smiled and said softly, "So you're telling me you want to save me like a candy bar?"

That memory always made me nostalgic and weepy, as did the others that followed one after the other like a ribbon of cutout paper dolls, mindlessly holding hands: the way he would take my hand in his in the darkness of a movie theater; the warm, knowing look in his eyes that would coax me out of a hesitation to talk; his extraordinary facility with the language of love that matched anything Marvell might have said about "world enough and time." And then there was the special way he would look at me when he came to pick me up for our dates. No sooner in the door, he would say, in an oddly shy way, "You look nice," managing to make it seem sincere each time. The husky edge to his voice when he said those words always made me feel as if we had just rolled over in a bed churned up by our lovemaking.

Once again, as I stared at his signature, the familiar scrawl evoked the look and feel of his hands, strangely delicate for a man. I could still feel their soft, pearly texture as I curled my hand over his. With the passing of the years, I would from time to time close my eyes to see whether I could summon up that tactile memory, and it never failed me. The touch of his hand on mine stayed with me far longer than any memory of his hand circling my breasts, caressing my face, or slipping between my thighs.

I sighed as I said to myself, *"He was the love of my life."* It was true, and I loved saying it, even though the relationship had been over for twenty-five years—perhaps *because* it had been over that long and I had the luxury of looking back on all my loves. I loved saying it because for so many years I thought love was something made up in Hollywood. Something Rita Hayworth, my childhood idol, had concocted. When we were in our first flush of romance, Dan, remembering what I had told him of my Rita Hayworth devotion, scoured the city to find me her signature poster, the one where she is seated and wearing a tight-fitting black negligée, tantalizing men with those voluptuous shoulders and teasing expression. But it wasn't just that as a young teenager I had assumed I might soon grow into such a body of my own (that was not to be), I was also drawn to Rita by what her movies showed her to be: as independent and smart as she was seductive and vulnerable. What really mattered in my adult years was that Dan—who accorded the great philosophers of the world far more importance than any Hollywood movie star, and rightly so—didn't belittle my childish attachment to the "Love Goddess," as she was called in her heyday. Instead, I knew that in embracing her, he was embracing me.

During that exhilarating, magical time, I was fully aware that I adored the image he had of me almost as much as I adored him. Dan managed to re-create me as everything I wanted to be—smart, perceptive, funny, and sexy. Rita could not have asked for more.

One evening, not long after we met, we went to one of our favorite cafes. The decor was romantic—festooned with plants and generally furnished in the lavish funky style left over from the sixties. We always looked to see if our favorite table was available. It was raised on a platform in the window facing the street. It was there where we felt our conversations could be private, where we could hold hands and probe souls. That evening we had barely sat down when he surprised me by reaching for my hand, sadness flooding his eyes and choking his voice, saying, "I could really hurt you, you know." He looked down, his hand still on mine; he seemed desolate beyond description. He then began haltingly to tell me how many women he had known and failed, simply because he could never hold on to the first flush of feeling.

As heady a time as it was for me, at that moment I did not know that he would turn out to be the love of my life. And so, I took his words lightly, coming back with some sassy response that made him laugh, and seemed to reassure him that either he need not worry about me or that I might be the exception to his track record. The truth is, until Dan, I had been the one to do the leaving. I guess my confidence stemmed from that and from my odd state of never having found the kind of love that leaves you bereft when it is taken away. But taken away it was. Not immediately, but, like a prophesy he was bound to fulfill, in a few years' time. Perhaps that was the pattern he knew so well: when his intense love was returned, it signaled the "end of the affair."

When it did finally happen, no amount of analyzing helped, of course. Discarded by the love of my life, like scores of women before me, I called and pleaded, called and cajoled, called and pretended to be casual, called and sobbed. Driving to his apartment late at night to throw raw eggs at his car—something I still can't believe I did—turned out to be of no use at all.

In the weeks that followed our final breakup, friends would try to soothe me with their leftover aphorisms, like "There's always another train coming down the track." Their clichés didn't work then, just as I doubt whether today's would work: "It's time to move on," or the vaguely spiritual, "Everything happens for a reason."

Now, a quarter century later, I still have check #1104, I still have his picture on my kitchen windowsill, I still have the rings and necklaces he gave me, and I still have the black leather jewelry case with a love poem slipped into its pocket. And on a lonely evening, I can still conjure up the smooth touch of his fingers on mine and see the sweet look of love in those intensely brown eyes.

As in the past, I return the check to the box where I found it, and put the box back in the closet where it will sit, indistinguishable from other boxes filled with bits and pieces of my past, until the next time. As I leave the room and return to the realities of the present, I have a ludicrous realization: the love of my life has, in fact, followed me everywhere. You might well say that Dan Friedman never left me.

Bedded Bliss

⚬ ROSE SOLOMON

Nearly ten years ago, to mark our anniversary, Sam proposed buying a new mattress.

"Twenty-five years is a long time, too long for the same mattress," he said, complaining that he'd been waking up with back pain.

I accepted his offer with mixed feelings. I loved our old mattress and its familiar geography. It had taken our passion a quarter century to carve the gentle hillocks and valleys. The worn mattress was testimony of our marital evolution, from our first frantic couplings to the more sustainable yet intense lovemaking of our prime. I would miss its soft compliance, its frayed piping, and the benign sag that kept us close throughout the night.

At the same time the seductive power of Sam's offer brought out the bride in me. I wanted new linens, too, and an eiderdown. No one but Sam knows what an avid bed-goer I am. I look forward to bedtime with the eagerness of an inveterate theater-goer. The play that I anticipate is not just the one that occurs between the sheets but also the Kodachrome continuum of dreams that occurs inside my head.

Sam likes to tease that my nights unfold much more eventfully than my days, and he is right. I often awake like a space traveler returning from a realm beyond earthly constraints, where past and future merge and I converse with the dead and the unborn. In one underwater dream I attended a family reunion at the bottom of our favorite swimming hole along the Truckee River. My relatives wore black dress clothes, not diving gear, and I kissed the grandfather and the great-grandparents I had never known. Often I wake up laughing, as I did when I dreamt my mother had written a best-seller entitled *What's in It for Me?*

My dreams taunt me with portent. I keep a notebook in which I try to decode cryptic dream messages. An eleven-digit phone number kept appearing in a spy thriller nightmare. It was the key to saving the world, but I could remember only three digits when I awakened. Another dream fragment delivered the secret of psychotherapy by fax machine, but the printout went back into the machine faster than I could read it. Still, these garbled messages give me hope that, with effort and awareness, life's mysteries can be understood, and I return home from my dream journeys with a pervasive sense of possibility.

Aroused by Sam's enticement, my dreams began to resemble Chagall paintings, full of flying beds that could soar and glide. The mattresses in my dreams sped like magic carpets, and I rode them lying stomach down, clinging to the edges. I mastered triple loops and learned to swoop low and hover, barely skimming the tops of people's heads.

潬 潬 潬

Since Sam is a comparative shopper, we set aside a whole Saturday to visit mattress showrooms. We quickly learned that there is no way to shop comparatively for a mattress because each store invents its own names for the merchandise. A Serta Perfect Sleeper Golden Elegance at Macy's might be a Serta Imperial Majesty or a Serta Midnight Lace Rhapsody at Mattress Express.

The confusion in labeling did not inhibit us long. Sam dove facedown into a Simmons pillow-top Countess Elite while I backed onto a Stearns and Foster Regency Inspiration. It turned out to be an inhospitable queen, far too stiff for even a one-night stand. I got up, passed a row of royals (Grand Duke Brandon, Squire Dewsbury, His Lordship Swindon, and the Matriarch II), and headed straight for the Sealy Posturepedic Presidential Maxima. No sooner had I stretched out and closed my eyes than I felt someone settle beside me. It was a white-haired stranger.

"Would you roll around?" he asked. "I want to feel it move."

I obligingly tossed and turned.

"Hey, honey," he called to his wife. "This one's pretty good."

A portly woman, heavier than her husband, joined us. The mattress didn't sag when she sat down to untie her shoes. I moved over to give her more room and spotted Sam two beds away bouncing with a young couple on a Sealy Pillowsoft Sauvignon.

"You should try this!" he called to me as a saleslady approached.

"Can I help you folks?"

The saleslady carried some sawed-off cross sections of mattresses to show the intricacies of construction. Many layers of foam and acrylic padding overlaid the metal springs.

"Where has all the cotton gone?" I wanted to know. None of the samples displayed the endearing cotton ticking of old. Instead, the demo models were covered with shiny polyesters full of metallic highlights. They looked like show-girls. They belonged in Las Vegas.

"Only motels order the cotton ticking," said the saleslady. "Bottom of the line."

Out of loyalty to our old mattress, we decided upon another Serta Perfect Sleeper, but this time the extra-firm Diamond Classic model. Though garbed in a garish blue and bronze brocade, its solidity promised a spartan sleep.

ॐ   ॐ   ॐ

Our last night on the old mattress, I dreamt in arithmetic. I was trying to figure out how old I'd be in another twenty-five years, when the new mattress would be the same age as our current one. In my dream I kept coming up with ninety-three, even though the correct answer was seventy-five, but both numbers felt equally old. My dream gave me a sneak preview of what ninety-three would feel like: I was so light that I didn't make a dent. I lay dry and brittle as straw, stranded in the middle of the new mattress that loomed bigger and flatter than Kansas. Its nearest edge was no more than a distant horizon, and I had to claw and grope my way just to reach it. When I finally swung my feet over the edge to stand, I moved as stiffly as a twig. The slightest breeze would topple me....

I awoke in tears. This was the bed of our youth! Our

babies were conceived on it! How could we give it away?

"We'll never muster the passion to break in a new one. It will be the bed of old age and worse: our deathbed!"

"Too late," said Sam. "It comes today. Besides, my back can't take another night in this hammock."

Mid-morning, Mattress Express rolled down the narrow street to our house. The truck was so high it nearly downed the power lines. The driver and his potbellied partner smelled of cigarettes as they marched upstairs to the bedroom. Their stocky, dirty hands bent the old mattress in half when they hauled it away. I nearly cried out when they tossed it onto the sidewalk. A neighbor dog strolled by and spent a long time sniffing it before he condescended to pee on one corner.

The delivery men unloaded the tightly swaddled new mattress set from the truck. First they carried up the box springs. Then, gasping for breath, they struggled around the bend in the stairs with the mammoth new mattress. After finally wedging it through the bedroom door, they unwrapped miles and miles of protective plastic and heaved the mattress onto the box springs.

I sat down to test it, alarmed to find that it had no give and that my feet didn't reach the floor.

"It's so high," I said, but my words were drowned out by the crinkling of the plastic that the men were hauling away.

The bed filled the room like a giant conquistador. The ceiling suddenly seemed very low and the walls much closer. The mattress's machine-stitched surface rippled with welts and puckers, unpleasant to touch. Its pseudo-brocade covering gave off a blue aura and a sharp, synthetic smell that was utterly foreign and faintly threatening, as if it were emitting a noxious gas.

My best option was to subdue the bed by making it. A struggle ensued. Though the old mattress pad and contour sheet were too small, I managed to wrestle them halfway over the bulging sides. By the time I finished layering the top sheet and covers, the bedspread hung not quite two-thirds of the way to the floor, exposing the box spring's underbelly, the ugly iron frame and its cheap plastic wheels. The pillows sat so high atop the stiffly made-up bed that they obscured the headboard. I stepped back from my work and appraised the bed's invasive bulk. A menacing stranger had entered our lives.

When Sam came home that night, he climbed aboard, lay back, and stared at the ceiling.

"You're right," he said. "The ceiling does seem awfully close. You usually exaggerate."

I heaved myself onto the bed and lay beside him.

"Doesn't your pelvis feel like it's being lifted above your head?"

"Sort of, but I think this will be better for my back."

We went to bed too disconsolate to consummate the new mattress that night or for many nights to come. Neither of us wanted to admit a mistake. The mattress was as unyielding as a park bench. It felt therapeutic, not at all conducive to reading or talking or cuddling. We kept to separate sides of the bed like hospital patients in traction. No position felt comfortable. The mattress's uneven surface impaled our bedclothes, and we woke often in a stranglehold of knotted nightshirts and twisted sheets. Worse, the layers of quilted foam didn't breathe and heated us to a sweaty simmer.

"Maybe we'll never have sex again," I mused aloud. Sam made no reply. His silence attested to our growing estrangement. Desire was evaporating, and I stopped dreaming.

        ✺   ✺   ✺

If our first bed had been the spring and summer of our marriage, this one was certainly the winter, and an early one at that. A raw chill gripped our hearts, and defensiveness set in. Talking late at the night in the stiff new bed, words led us astray and punctured the dark in strange, staccato bursts. *You've changed…You don't touch me…I'm not sure you like me. We never…You always…I can't…I'm not thirty anymore…You're being unrealistic. Change happens…No, no. We're not that old. I'm not ready…Maybe we should see a therapist?…*

As a peace offering, Sam bought a huge synthetic fleece to fit over the hostile mattress. It ameliorated the situation enough for us to sleep without strangling and to reach out for each other again. But bed was not the lazy, inviting place it once had been. We woke earlier and got up, preferring almost any upright activity to lolling posturepedically in bed.

Once sleep became possible again, strange new dreams took shape. Unlike the uplifting dreamscapes of old that I had so eagerly embraced, these dreams lurked in the shadows like stalkers: colossal tsunamis rose up from the Pacific to engulf all of San Francisco, sweeping away my parents' house and everything familiar from my past; unfriendly squatters usurped my current home while my in-laws sat at the dining table waiting for me to serve them a dinner I hadn't yet cooked or even shopped for; men in gray flannel suits closed in on me at a bankers' cocktail party as one of them turned into a wolf and loped away on all fours toward my house to eat my children; during a ladies' luncheon on a houseboat, I saw a giant python slither up onto the deck and swallow my friend's first grandchild before I could stop it; a garden hose, left running on my desk, soaked my manuscripts and washed away all the words I had ever written. In my nightmares I triaged train wrecks and gory highway collisions and narrowly escaped several fiery plane crashes. Helplessly, I watched my daughter's skin peel off her body as she toppled from her bike across rough asphalt.

During brief remissions from these dreams, I found no respite. Sam's recurring nightmare Nazis for the first time infiltrated my side of the bed and pursued me with machine-gun fire. One of them cornered me and held a shotgun to my crotch. "Go ahead," I said. "It's already dead."

I woke Sam, told the dream, and asked him to keep his Nazis on his side of the bed.

"I can't control them," was all he said.

We slept back to back, turning away from each other. During this bleak period, I was developing an aversion to sex, which revealed itself most disturbingly in a dream about a business leaders' banquet. As a member of a board of directors, consisting only of men, I had been invited to a formal dinner in a high-rise hotel. We filed past the hatcheck girl, and I saw a sign that read, *Gentlemen, please check your genitals at the door.* I watched in fascination as the men unzipped their tuxedo trousers, took out their genitals, and hung them on meat hooks on the wall. There were so many varieties and colors, with no way of predicting who had what. Some very short men had enormous clusters, while some of the very tallest and most mesomorphic had tiny ones. Some very pale white men had pink or lavender genitals, while some of the darker men sported blues, grays, and browns. Of course, none of the penises was erect. Each hung dejectedly from its hook, some trying to hide in the folds of their scrotums, which seemed to come in even more varieties than the penises. Some looked almost taut, so large and tightly packed were the testicles, while others hung as lank and loose as fine Italian leather purses. Upon close examination, a delicate filigree of veins and vessels could be seen on most of the scrotums, reminiscent of the Arabic scripture found in friezes of the Royal Mosque Masjid-i Shah in Esfahān, Iran.

Once the male genitals had been safely checked at the door, we moved single-file into the banquet room and took our places at the white, satin clothed table. Without their genitalia, the gentlemen were all smiles and sociability. We conversed benignly on any subject at all. I was struck by what sweet people they could be without the burden of their sexual equipment, and I secretly gloated that all mine was intact and safely stored internally, far from public view.

If I ever dreamt of Sam during this unlibidinous period, it was with such longing that I would awaken wet from crying. In one dream, I was sitting on the cold steps outside a temple rehearsing my vows for our remarriage ceremony. I ached to make a significant speech about all the things he meant to me, but the notes in my hand were years old, on yellowed binder paper, and utterly wrong. In another dream, the master of ceremonies at an awards banquet asked everyone to drink to "the person we all love most"… my husband's lover. A tall, slender, naked woman in her thirties rose to take the mike and regaled us with a raunchy song. She was un-self-conscious about her nakedness and seemed not to mind the sideburns on her inner thighs and the trail of hair that grew toward her belly button. I envied her self-acceptance, wished that I were his lover, and felt sad that our truth had been exposed. At the same time, Sam sat with his arm around me in the dream. He kindly explained all the inside jokes. When I woke up and told Sam the dream and how I wished I were the lover, he said he did, too.

🚲   🚲   🚲

What makes a dark time pass? Was it the inevitable change of season, hormone replacements, an acceptance of fate, a new exercise regimen? Or a different mattress?

Quite unexpectedly, we found ourselves in a mattress showroom. We had just eaten an overlarge lunch at Zuni Cafe with my brother and his wife, when enormous somnolence engulfed us. As we stumbled out of the restaurant onto Market Street, we noticed the McRoskey Airflex Mattress Factory up the block. We staggered in and collapsed on the beds.

It was nothing like home. I landed on the Gentle Firm Comfort and found heaven. The handmade construction cradled my bones like the embrace of a loving mother. The soft cotton ticking and layers of natural padding gave instant succor. Sam and I could lie together in a friendly embrace without feeling like we were falling off a park bench. The four of us lay long and quietly on the sample beds like accident victims resuscitating in an emergency room. Soft moans came from my brother who floated upon the Extra Gentle Comfort, which he dubbed the "Posture Pudding."

"I think we should call it the 'La Brea,'" said his wife, and they ordered two on the spot.

Sam and I deferred our decision, going home first to see if our mattress was as hateful as we remembered. It was. Because each McRoskey mattress is custom-made by hand, we had to wait three months for ours to be delivered.

The first night on our Gentle Firm Comfort, Sam and I swam into each other's arms feeling as buoyant as divers in a tropical sea. In my dreams, I began to fly again, this time by inhaling deeply and willing myself to levitate. On my belly, moving my arms and legs in a breaststroke, I swam through space. I could jump from seven-story buildings and stay aloft without falling, and swing on a rope as high as I wanted to go, higher than treetops, level with flying kites. I dreamt of dogs, an auspicious topic for me, signifying spontaneity, joy, and affirmation. Big, black ones barked and snarled outside my bedroom window until I let them in. They ran gaily through the house and out the front door to return again and again through the bedroom window. In another dream, hiking up a steep mountain with my dog, we came upon a horse and rider, usually a source of terror for my dog. But in the dream he turned to me and said, "Nice horse."

In my new night journeys, abundance triumphs over fear. From the folds of a magical new tampon, jewels and charms tumble onto my bathroom tile. I discover that I have three vaginas and that Sam's penis has grown a fur coat that makes it look like a friendly, gray mole. I do not want him to give it to the hatcheck girl. What an absurd delight is this strange and fleeting bed life! A new season has dawned, a rich harvesttime of life. Our McRoskey mattress heralds autumn, ripe with earthly delight, and we are hunkering down under the covers to make it through another winter.

III. Flesh in Flux

We are mortal. More to the point, we are old! This truth
continually takes us by surprise: When one Lady gets her
hair cut, clippings sift to the floor like snow. She watches it
accumulate before realizing, in disbelief, that it is hers. She is
going white! Another laments that her spreading thighs spill
helplessly over her spartan swivel desk chair that once con-
tained her so neatly. During a headstand at yoga, another
one's face falls down over her eyes, nearly blocking her view.

And the doctors we feel we've known forever: how fragile they suddenly seem. One Lady's gynecologist holds her
hands in his as they discuss declining libido (hers), elevated
PSA (his), and the pros and cons of eternal hormone replacement therapy. We are all old friends, facing the inevitable.

Flesh of our flesh, when did you give in so completely to
the laws of gravity? Why do you surrender so quietly? Who
are you with your papery skin, soft wattles, delicate wrinkles?
Are these lacy networks of purple spider veins on our legs a
map to somewhere? When, exactly, did all this happen?

The innards haven't undergone such evolutions: the
mouth, the tongue, the gut are in working order. The heart
still beats. The lungs breathe. The stomach cries out for
more. A kiss is still a kiss. Deep down we are the same obedient children, the defiant adolescents, the hardworking
young mothers, the amazed new grandmothers.

The exterior and the interior have never been more out of
whack, except perhaps in youth when our contours changed

into women before the rest of us did. Now our bodies are deserting us just as the age of wisdom promises to arrive.

Nature is more kind and egalitarian than we give her credit for. Although she doles out youth more generously than old age, for our middle years she mercifully alters our sight, handing out presbyopia to all. And finally, in old age, Nature is a great leveler: the beauty, speed, and prowess that may have distinguished and divided us is fading. She challenges us to find humanity and meaning elsewhere.

Louder Than Life

❧ BERNADETTE VAUGHAN

As far back as I can remember, I have experienced pictur-
esque twists in acoustic reality. This tendency finally led my
children, then aged eight and six, to suggest diplomatically
that it was time for me to consult an audiologist. We had
been listening to the Beatles, whose lyrics require attention.

"What does he mean?" I asked the children. *"And send a
rubber band in his face?"*

They exchanged meaningful glances. Then my daughter
said carefully, "What he means, Mama, is what he said: *hand
in hand with another man in his place."*

This mishearing was a matter of no surprise to any of us.
My lightly off-kilter appreciation of what was being said was
nothing if not familiar. Language, to me, has always been an
adventure, a veritable *Cirque du Soleil* of drifting smoke and
fun-house mirrors, and I often have the feeling that I am the
only inhabitant of a private planet on which all communication is in code. This idiosyncrasy is best explained by the fact
that my mother's native tongue was French, peppered with
the dialects she learned as a child in Madagascar, Vietnam,
and Senegal, which she freely deployed while I was growing
up. Her English, comparatively late adopted and forced to

pass, on its way to expression, first through her own world-view and then through a four-way language filter, charged the simplest statement with enough energy to make the words erupt in flight, sending them wheeling and tumbling across my eidetic imagination like flocks of Technicolor birds.

"It is about five miles," she said once, describing the way to our house, "as the bee crows."

I attempted to brush the Beatles incident aside, although I had to admit that for some years I had received rumor of the world at a soft remove, as though I had a sofa cushion draped over my head. But the children were adamant and campaigned so energetically for a hearing test that I allowed myself, after several missteps, to be swept into the great, chaste, uncompromising embrace of science.

I invested in a hearing aid.

The hearing aid in question is a streamlined, convoluted, slightly repellent object that fits right inside the ear (actually, in my case both ears). It has an amorphous, embryonic quality, shiny and pink, reminiscent of a newborn marsupial on its way to completion in the maternal pouch. As someone once said about English cars, it would delight someone afflicted with a bad case of the itsy-bitsies: everything about it is *teensy*—switch, carrying case, tools required for maintenance, batteries.

Even after all this time, I still can't respond calmly to these batteries. There is too much in the universe that cannot be explained, and much of it involves electricity. I have nothing but sympathy for that aunt of James Thurber's who sat around all day paralyzed with worry that electricity might be leaking through the house. So here we have a battery, brazen and unstable, inserted into a device designed to inhabit an aperture leading directly to my brain. I was not, am not, prepared to be relaxed about this, although I have grown used to it after ten or so years. But suppose something were to short out? Would I explode or merely smolder? As my massage therapist, hurriedly blotting tears from my face before they could slide into my ears and cause an eruption of sizzling blue flame, said cheerfully the other day, "I can just see the headlines: WOMAN VAPORIZES ON MASSAGE TABLE." I still think I should carry the bomb squad's hotline number in my wallet, along with the organ donor's card and *Who to Contact in Case of Emergency* and wonder if I am doomed to go through life feeling like something a group of fervid political extremists might leave under a seat at Heathrow Airport.

When outfitted with my brand-new, battery-powered, just-activated hearing aids, I left my audiologist's office, I remember a profound intimation of change. And rightly so. Suddenly, I had hearing as sharp as that of a fennec. My life was awash with noise. I could hear *everything*. I was appalled. The ether, formerly benign, now assaulted me with small, jarring explosions. Dazed and apprehensive, I listened to a barrage of retorts, of pops and bangs and a peculiar series of overlapping metallic swishes—as if someone were flinging armloads of wire coat hangers through a line of puddles—brought about, evidently, by the simple actions of crossing the street, unlocking the car, settling myself in the driver's seat, and turning on the ignition. By mistake I switched on the windshield wipers and was assaulted by the sound of vast, powerful wings beating throughout the vehicle, rather in the manner of Dolby Sensurround. The effect was huge, expellant, full of whooshing and grunting sounds, as if the Angel of Death had taken on the Dove of Peace in Olympic Gold Medal Class no-holds-barred wrestling in the backseat.

Inhibiting a tendency to duck, I somehow made it home without mishap and came to a clashing Bronze Age halt in the driveway. The car door, and then the front door, opened and closed like earthquake and thunderclap. The water I shakily drew from the faucet roared forth and pounded into the glass, exquisitely reproducing the sound of the Reichenbach Falls. Moving through the house, I heard my footsteps crackling on the carpet like wildfire devouring a forest; I flushed the toilet and stood aghast as a tsunami blasted through the walls.

This was not the scenario I had written at all. The way I had it, the improvement was going to be selective, rather like one of those Sonnheiser contrivances you get at the theater, that render the actors perfectly audible and the audience, with its rustling, coughing, shuffling and creaking, as silent as something preserved in formaldehyde. Instead, what I had was havoc and the baying of the hounds of war. I could have stood right up with Henry V at Harfleur and terrified the citizenry into quiescence.

Evidently, monstrous forces were loose in the world. Things got worse as the day progressed: the most innocuous actions, flicking a light switch, placing a cup on a saucer, striking a match, resounded like Acts of God. *Good Lord!* Was this what other people, *good* people with *normal* hearing, the ones I wistfully sought to emulate, lived with all the time? How on Earth did they stand it? And what about those beeps, chirps, and squeaks—it's called *feedback*—that emanate from the contraption in the course of close physical encounters? It rapidly became apparent that for derailing a tender, cheek-to-cheek moment—or any moment of head and neck erotica—ear trumpets are without peer. Lovers, long-term or new or returning, start back as if stung; thereafter they approach with caution. The whole situation was hideously uncomfortable and augured ill for future bliss.

Demoralized, I began to question the wisdom of taking on a hearing aid. It seemed that I had made an expensive mistake that possibly had its origins in mere vanity. Had things really been so bad, before? Perhaps all I needed to do was return the device with a note of thanks and accept the status quo. But that was not a comfortable solution. There's a responsibility attached to having five senses, as anyone who has survived the Last Sacrament, during the course of which each one is anointed and forgiven, will attest; you don't cavalierly abandon one of them if you have any choice in the matter.

I sat down to examine my plight, summoning the rule of thumb I rely upon in moments of perplexity: *when in doubt, review.*

The official diagnosis of hearing loss—the one that took place shortly after the Beatles incident—came from a doctor who belonged to the George Bush Senior School of Verbal Communication. He finished his examination and summoned me into his office.

"Inner ear," he said. "Nerve damage."

He stared at me accusingly for a while and then said, "Too young for it. Childhood illness. Probably."

But which illness? Mumps, measles, chickenpox? I had malaria as a child, repeatedly, because I lived in the tropics. Could that cause nerve damage to the inner ear?

The question would have to wait. Right now, I was enchanted by the notion of being too young for any medical condition, since at the time, physicians confronted with female patients over the age of forty tended visibly to disintegrate and plummet into a downward spiral of gibberish that included about five intelligible words—"Valium" and "menopause" being two of them. Bravely, for I am mortally afraid of knives, I asked if there were any miracles of modern surgery that might be applicable to my condition. My physician gazed at me in glassy horror, like some timid woodland creature suddenly confronted with a gamekeeper's beaters.

"Irreversible," he said.

He opened a drawer and stared morosely into it. I thought he was going to produce a panacea on the spot, hand it to me in its packet, like a drug sample. But no.

"Hearing aid," he said.

Our interview was over. I left his office light-headed with shock. Hearing aid? *Quelle effronterie!* We're talking about a pantomime prop! How could I incorporate such a blot on my self-image?

Baby-boomer presidents and their rock-and-roll auditory appendages notwithstanding, diminished hearing is still not socially acceptable the way failing sight is. There is nothing covertly funny about a pair of spectacles perched on the nose; they might be unmistakable evidence of decreptitude but they are also a fashion statement, an accessory that can pull the edges of a personality into focus. But hearing aids?

No. These carry distinctly vaudeville connotations, holding
their own with pratfalls, dropped pants, and mother-in-law
jokes. Also, being rather deaf (or, as the desperately fragrant
circumlocution would have it, *hard of hearing*) seems to
elicit far more exasperation from the world at large than total
deafness. This last, I think, is seen as a bona fide, card-carry-
ing affliction, an unmistakable cross that must be borne, and
while often evoking a reaction of cave-dwelling terror, it
does tend to be addressed with an attempt at compassion.
Partial deafness, on the other hand, tends to be viewed as an
infuriating choice, one that anybody with an iota of native
wit or social conscience would choose to reverse.

So I prevaricated. I grew more and more adept at reading
lips, painstakingly observing facial expressions for clues to a
conversation's content and direction. I developed a reputa-
tion for being an unusually attentive listener. My antennae,
already finely tuned from a lifetime of dealing with my
mother's baroque linguistic approach, became minutely
responsive. Shamelessly, I dissembled; I became expert at
producing an appropriate signal—a small, noncommittal
sound, an eloquent eyebrow, a grimace, a shrug—even when
I hadn't the foggiest notion of what was being said. Then
matters took a turn for the worse, and a new diagnosis
revealed that my upper register began where other people's
ended. No high-pitched or even medium-pitched sounds
were penetrating at all. Down deep in the bass-baritone
ranges, though, I heard rather well.

"Hearing aid!" boomed the new doctor jovially. He was
an extrovert and I capitulated. Oh, what the hell. Why not?

There followed some thought-provoking visits to the

audiologist, who studied the diagnosis—to me it looked like an elaborate game of tic-tac-toe, all noughts and crosses—then filled my ears with warm liquid plastic. When it hardened, he said, he would have two facsimiles—ordinance survey maps, if you will—of my inner ears. These, he said, would be fashioned into discreet little devices barely visible to the naked eye. I tried to put my faith in the facts as presented, but I knew in my heart that the situation was made-to-order for God's lamentable sense of humor. I'd studied that diagram of ear geography on the wall of his office and I could see no persuasive evidence that those twin streams of plastic, hardening as they advanced, would do anything but meet in the middle, merge, solidify, and cut me off forever from all contact with the part of my brain that responds to the command *"Now hear this!"*

Or maybe some other unexpected reaction would occur among those drums and shells, a first-ever occurrence, a miracle, the sort of thing that keeps the medical profession humble. Perhaps, along with that *oops!* that patients rarely hear because we are either anesthetized or, as I was at this point in the proceedings, stone-deaf when the near miss occurs, there would be an epiphany, a vision received by the Ear, Nose, and Throat Brigade with an awed, collective gasp: Phenomena as mysterious and evanescent as memories, materializing like flies in amber! Casts of the lineaments of my soul!

I might make it into the *National Enquirer*.

None of this happened, of course. The plastic hardened and was removed; a couple of weeks later I was summoned back for final adjustments to the completed devices. Then I took them home and began my struggle to incorporate all those catastrophic associations, all that apocalypse and deluge, into my daily life.

For ten years I thought all was well. But at a recent Kensington Ladies Erotica Society meeting a close misunderstanding of the Beatles kind left me suspecting, with a sinking heart, that a vertiginous plunge in my already compromised upper register had occurred.

What happened was this. The Ladies had finished dinner—an excellent German presentation of fish and apples prepared by Sabina—and were about to embark, as has always been our custom, on the Reading Aloud part of the evening. This is the part of our ritual that I love. The sinful chocolate cake was cut and distributed; the raspberry coulis applied generously with a soup ladle; the wine bottles were drained and set aside and coffee was poured. Some of us leaned back in our chairs, expansively, but with every critical nerve honed to mustard keenness. Some of us put our heads down on our arms, in true Story Time at kindergarten fashion, transfixed on a drift into fantasyland. Susan began to read, we listened attentively, and then… *"He told me how compelling he found the freezing scent of my hamstrings....*

I was utterly charmed and dreamily repeated the sentence. When the shrieks of mirth finally came under control, it was made clear that Susan's hamstrings were not at issue, not by a long shot; what was compelling to her protagonist, she explained, was *the freesia scent of her hand cream.*

Later, learned pronouncements decreed that my hearing has not deteriorated in ten years, that the problem is doubtless merely mechanical. I think this means that my hearing aid may have become sclerotic from years of service and I need to call in an ENT version of Roto-Rooter. Or replace my discreet little *aides oreilles* with a couple of those infinitely more accurate, externally flaunted, in-your-face, I'm-Deaf-and-I'm-Proud, digital ear trumpets that are now recommended for the auditorily challenged. Or perhaps my laconic physician was on target and the quinine I was given as a child to ward off the dislocating malaria did affect my hearing. My early memories, after all, are saturated not just with the sights and smells and tastes, but with the magical, rhythmical sounds of French West Africa. It makes sense that, as I grow older, my mind, body, and spirit might collaborate to force an examination of my earlier life.

All this may well be.

But there is something inescapably familiar about that freezing hamstrings episode. It was too vivid, too enchanting, and its effects—that immediate acceptance of the extraordinary, the unquestioning attempt *to make sense of it*—summon from my heart a persuasive murmur that there is no problem, none at all. I'm simply reverting to type, I'm swimming backward, a frog reverting to a tadpole. We learn language at such an early age, mirroring the speakers around us at so many infinitesimal levels, receiving and responding as befits our birthright. *Thou art thy mother's glass...* Perhaps the reason why my mother's language, splattering so vividly across her unique communicative canvas, spilling onto mine, caught and held me, waiting for my advancing in years to release me once more into a familiar cacophony of perception, was that she, too, was hardwired for a figurative view of the world.

"*Cher ami,*" she said to my father on one occasion, "your words run off my back like duck's water."

Well, I'm just going to lie back and enjoy whatever it is I hear next. These are the days of miracle and wonder, as Paul Simon thoughtfully reminds us, and anyway, I like my versions better. What a poetic, wonder-filled, color-drenched world they conjure up! And what perfect sense it all makes to me.

Dust to Dust

✦ ROSE SOLOMON

Today while cleaning out a deep closet, I discover a museum of sexual allurements stashed in a Thai silk lingerie case, a Smithsonian of feminine snares:

~ A black, strapless Merry Widow, great-grandmother of the Wonderbra, (though far crueler, with vertical bones to the waist), wanting to prop up my wares for formal viewing, an engineering feat at any age.

~ Two lace garter belts, flesh-toned, with pearl rosettes below the navel, rousing from their long retirement eager to clasp my hips like octopuses, elastic tentacles slithering against my thighs.

~ Seamed stockings sleeping in zippered pockets beside sanitary napkin belts (remember them?), and snap-on foam shoulder pads springing from their confinement like falsies.

~ The baby blue chiffon nightgown my mother gave me for my wedding night, still resting in peace in its solitary compartment, an eternal virgin.

How lovingly I stockpiled these accoutrements to convince myself of my own desirability, assuming I would someday live out their lacy, cinematic promise. But the hot breath of real life caught me unprepared every time. Only my diaphragm, hiding like a clam in its pink plastic shell, got any wear. When I touch it, oh so gently, my finger leaves a gaping hole. It has turned into a potato chip.

Waiting

CLAUDIA MORTON

Waiting with chrysanthemums,
   which wish you long life,
Longing with wine,
   for your life's friendship
October skies summering
   into November—
Winter weather waiting
   under the leaves.

Now you're here, embraced
   and glowing—
Saying, though, you've felt
   homesick lately
Knowing no good reason, just
   the gnawing
Unspecific loneliness of still
   having breath,
As a friend died too quick
   for thought.

That yearning for a safer time,
    I know it—
We dreamers often dream it
    in our autumn.
Then everyone we loved
    was living;
Nothing waited in the wings
    but life.

Now we know it's not that
    easy, living,
Losing comes more suddenly
    than gain.
Still we're laughing, glad
    to have each other
And another year of loving—
    even age.

Love Is a Many-Gendered Thing

& ROSE SOLOMON

Last Monday my husband, Sam, and I celebrated the neutering of our pup, Meeker, by going out for sushi in Rockridge. Not that we were glad to see Meeker lose his balls, but the overnight stay at the vet's gave us our first free evening since we had brought him home four months earlier.

We are stymied and exhausted by Meeker, a border collie who mistrusts all new experiences. He hates to leave the house, which he regards as the only safe sanctuary. It takes two of us, cajoling all the way, just to walk him half a block in our quiet residential neighborhood. Forget marathon goals like getting all the way around the block! Our private trainer thinks we're making progress—Meeker no longer bolts for home when a car approaches—but we have never worked so hard for so little. Raising our children and previous dogs seems effortless by comparison. I wonder if this is how old age feels—tired and discouraged.

The other diners around us talk loudly, nonstop. They look impossibly young. They have so much thick, bright hair, dark eyebrows, taut skin.

"Why do they have to pierce and tattoo it?" Sam asks.

"Because it's too perfect," I say.

I inspect the beautiful array of young couples of all races and combinations who are sitting nearby. Our adult children would criticize me for staring, but in their absence I am free of censorship. I feast my curiosity on the many pairs of women dressed like me, in rain gear and wilderness wear. On this cold winter night I am bundled in a down vest, a black polypro turtleneck, and black fleece pants. This has been my uniform ever since Meeker's arrival, which coincided with the drenching onset of El Niño. I hike with him in the hills first thing each day, no matter how wet. Like a firefighter responding to an alarm, I bound out of bed, throw on warm underlayers, boots, and slicker and drive Meeker to a quiet trailhead, far from city congestion. He leaps from the car, the eager, confident dog I want him to be.

Only now, as I survey the women in their jeans and boots and spiky hairdos, do I realize that, like them, I am Rockridge lesbian chic. Sam agrees. He says he likes me this way. No, I am too bulky, I tell him. I look more like the padded BAMM man, the mock attacker whom women learn to beat. Sam and my daughter have been hounding me to enroll in a BAMM (Bay Area Model Mugging) self-defense course. They worry that I am too polite. The world is becoming a more dangerous place, and I refuse to acknowledge this. My daughter warns that perfectly ordinary looking people can be vicious criminals. Some might be considered good-looking. Think of serial murderers Ted Bundy, Jeffrey Dahmer, and Cary Stayner. She says I will open the front door to rapists and robbers. I will invite them in for tea and chocolate chip cookies. And then what will I do? How will I fight them off? As it is, I don't even have the strength or authority to get Meeker to obey NO! and OFF!, not even for a liver treat. My forearms and hands are covered with wounds from his needle-sharp puppy teeth.

I squint at Sam through my bad eye, the one that hasn't had cataract surgery yet, and think how handsome and different he looks from the sharp-boned boy he was thirty-three years ago. He is bigger and soft-edged, a man and a half through this eye. He never used to have any flesh on him. I like how he has filled out, how his forehead has expanded as his hair has receded, how the white in his hair shines. In his big new parka he looks as indomitable as the padded attackers that BAMM teaches women to resist.

My "good" eye is closed shut with poison oak, one of the hazards of allowing Meeker to run off-leash in the hills through the underbrush. Sam is getting it, too, on his hands and wrists. He asks if I've enrolled yet in the BAMM training.

I tell him Meeker is my self-defense course right now. He pushes me beyond civilized limits. I shriek, I swat, I bellow, and regret these outbursts when I do. I don't have the energy to take on another project, especially not a man-beating one. I say I'd rather learn t'ai chi.

"That won't protect you," Sam says, shaking his heads, the blurry one in front and its haloed twin behind.

"You're a husband and a half," I say, wanting to divert him from his fears and demons. I describe what I am seeing. I do not add that soon he will be more than a husband and a half when he retires at the end of this year. I've grown protective of my time and space. I can't imagine his presence at home every day all day. Life will be a string of Sundays, the day I suspend my own activities to drift along with his. It's comfortable and classic, being the amiable companion, the willing wife, but every day? When Sunday is over, I've lost momentum. My ambition stalls. The story I'd been writing two days before is no longer compelling. It would be so easy to abandon it.

If every day were Sunday, I'd never get out of the kitchen. One meal would blur into the next. Diversions would replace intentions. We'd do errands together, like old people. Hit Kmart for new batteries, then Safeway for the two-for-one toilet paper sale. We'd clip coupons and be first in line for Red Lobster's early bird senior special at 5:00 P.M. A car lube would be a big occasion, and a visit from an appliance repairman a noteworthy commotion. I fear Sam will want to travel, but I have no wanderlust nor much other kind of lust. I don't even lust for lust.

Through my cloudy lens I watch Sam scratch the rash that's appearing on his arms, then rub his eyes.

"Be careful. You'll spread it."

He is exhausted, less resilient than he used to be. Worries about his sickest patients rob his sleep. He's been waking at four or five. I feel him tugging at the covers, getting up to take aspirin. By daybreak, dread of what the day holds in store has worn him down. He looks haggard before he's left the house. An irritation as un-life-threatening as poison oak takes a bigger toll than it should.

We stop talking. I'm afraid he's giving up on Meeker, giving up too easily on everything. I'm scared he'll die long before me or suffer a debilitating illness. Will I become his full-time caretaker earlier than I expect? I wonder if all along I've been training for this strange, disquieting time—his retirement and the new selves we are becoming. Will I harden and nag as he softens and slowly dissolves, both of us transforming into a Thurber cartoon couple?

"Remember Jimmy and Francesca Rumford?" I ask, reaching across the table to pour more sake into his cup. "Do you think we're getting to be like them?"

We used to see Jimmy and Francesca at my grandmother's dinner parties shortly after we were married. Well into their seventies then, Francesca had the deep voice, the beard, the height, and the short hair. Jimmy was diminutive with perfect, hairless skin and a high-pitched giggle. Francesca swore and relished dirty jokes. Though their sexes seemed to have switched, they appeared a perfectly balanced pair.

Before my grandmother's parties, we'd rehearse in the privacy of our car, "Remember: Jimmy's the man, Francesca's the woman."

Now Sam is laughing. He hunches over in his parka with shoulders shaking. I haven't seen him let go like this in ages. I empty my cup and feel the sake slide warm and thrilling down my throat.

"You'd like it, wouldn't you, if I strutted some new stuff," I say, "wore a tongue stud, tied you to the bed, and pretended you're the BAMM man?"

"Yeah, that would be nice, for a change...."

"If only I could stay awake long enough."

These days sleep is the greater seducer. It's the culprit that keeps me from becoming the sexual instigator he'd like me to be. I realize how much he needs a change, how willingly he'd switch roles, at least for now. One of us needs to be the initiator, and while I watch the vibrant, confident women laughing and chattering at nearby tables, I decide it had better be me. I reach into my handbag for a pen and write myself a note to sign up for the BAMM training as a start. Then, on the paper placemat, I sketch out a cartoon rendition of our new transsexual selves. I draw a newly neutered Meeker flanked by a BAMM-ma'am me, with spiky hair and bulging biceps, and a fleshy, androgynous Sam, complete with wattles, a sagging bosom, and shoulder-length curls. I turn the place-mat to show him.

"Look, we're a New Age trinity."

His tired eyes crinkle into a smile, and his big, warm hand closes over mine. We pour more sake and sigh. Anything to make change palatable. Anything to stay connected.

Salad Days: A Recipe (or Three)

ℰ THE LADIES

If one gets to live long enough, life brings us full circle. We Ladies are finding ourselves back in our salad days, only this time youth's inexperience has been replaced by age's cantankerous rebellion. Sexy cooks are lazy cooks, we're learning. We are tossing out old formats and playing with the new. Like hunter-gatherers, we spend more time browsing the local farmers' markets for quick and easy edibles rather than slave in the kitchen. The family china and crystal stay in their cupboards while we crowd like sows in heat around a table laden with colorful, inventive salads that are meals in themselves. This way we can eat, read aloud, drink, and talk without anyone having to leave the room to run back and forth to the kitchen, all the while wailing, "Don't say a word until I come back...."

VOULEZ-VOUS COUSCOUS?

This recipe is so easy it's sinful. While it can be an accompaniment for leafy salads and meats, it's colorful enough to stand alone. It is a favorite of Naughty Nell, who gets all her cooking done well in advance.

Pour 1¹/2 half cups of boiling water over 1¹/2 cups of couscous. Leave them in the privacy of a covered pot for at least 5 minutes. Then fluff.

Add a mixture of ¹/2 cup currants, ¹/2 cup golden raisins, 1 bunch finely sliced scallions, 1 finely chopped red bell pepper, and ¹/2 can garbanzos (rinsed, with skins removed).

Last, toss everything together in this riotous dressing: ¹/3 cup olive oil, 3 tablespoons vinegar, juice of half a lemon, 4 pressed garlic cloves, 2 tablespoons curry powder, and salt and black pepper to taste. If you want it hotter, add a little cayenne. It makes a great leftover, too. Just right for a midnight raid on the refrigerator.

ELVIRA'S HEALDSBURG SALAD

I had been in my new North Bay town for just a short time when I took an East Bay friend to the sweet little (no-longer-there) cafe in the back of a bookstore. Surrounded by books, we were deep into our catching-up conversation when our salads arrived. One bite, and we both stopped talking to proclaim its wonders...the contrasting textures of apples and oranges and pears—oh, those pears!—the nutty surprise of the walnuts, the soft sharpness of the cheese, the slippery tang of the poppy seed dressing. This salad may not be exotic, but in it I found rapture. Because of its light fruitiness, it is equally satisfying at the opening or closing of a meal. *La voici!*

Cut up pears, oranges, and apples into your favorite salad bowl. Make the poppy seed dressing by mixing together 1 cup olive oil, ¹/3 cup cider vinegar, ¹/4 cup sugar (or to taste), salt to taste, 1 teaspoon dry mustard, and 2 tablespoons poppy seeds. Allow it to have its way with the fruit while you toast walnuts, shred white Cheddar (preferably Wisconsin), and prepare lettuce for the time of its life. Unite all and go mad with pleasure!

SABINA'S GERMAN POTATO SALAD

When I was growing up, my family ate potatoes every day—boiled, fried, mashed, and disguised in casseroles, dumplings, soups, and salads. In winter, I brought them to the kitchen from the dark, damp root cellar, where they'd sprouted lanky greens reaching up to the tiny window. In the spring, our school class would be commandeered to the fields to deliver the young potato plants from voracious bugs. In October, we helped the farmers dig the new crop out of the loamy soil, and we'd roast a big batch in the burning potato weeds.

My mother picked the tiny baby potatoes for her salad, adding nothing but fresh-cut chives and parsley and home-made mayonnaise with a dash of wine vinegar. I liked the more robust salad that I tasted first at our neighbors' house. (My North German father frowned on my mother's attempts to bring the pulpy, soft potatoes of South German cuisine to our table.) Naturally I endowed this most humble peasant dish with irreverent, if not illicit, ambience. Because of its secret potential to make a plain dish exotic and to put even an uninspired cook in the mood to try something wild, it has been my favorite recipe ever since (along with sauerkraut and schuebling).

I begin by selecting six mature russet potatoes. Each must fit comfortably into my hand, so that I can rub my fingers over the skin. A little roughness or a bulge here and there is fine, as long as the body lies firm and resilient in my grip.

No clock can tell you when your boiling potatoes are truly ready; observe them closely. Watch until the skins begin to pop. There's always a quick popper who wants to come first or a long boiler who requires a patient cook. Allow your potatoes to cool enough for you to handle them again—the hotter they are, the easier they will be to peel and slice. By then they will be longing for the pungent dressing you've prepared.

For the dressing mix 1/2 cup water and 1/2 cup wine vinegar and bring to a boil. Chop up a large onion and sprinkle it over the potato slices. Pour on the hot vinegar, add salt and pepper to taste, and mix everything well with salad oil.

Over the years, I have added a lot of new ingredients to this basic recipe. Diced cucumbers (drained of excess water), green onions, fresh herbs in season, and sour cream or yogurt to add moisture. Lately I've become enamored of Chinese greens, so I chop up some leftover mustard greens (steamed and drained) to dress up my potato salad with yet another shocking new taste.

Body Surfing

&️ NELL PORT

Here I am in my sixties, weighing more than I ever
have—including the day I delivered twins—and for the first
time I feel like celebrating my body.

I've gone through my whole life being hypercritical of
my physique. Either I believed I was too fat—most of the
time—or too thin—once, for about six months when I was a
twenty-five-year-old grad student. (Every day I ate just one-
seventh of a sweet roll for breakfast and one-quarter cup of
cottage cheese with one ring of pineapple for lunch to get
that way.)

But yesterday I looked at myself in the mirror with gentler, more loving eyes and decided to inventory the parts of
my body I like best. For starters, I told myself as I raised my
chin and threw back my shoulders, I've got great tits. Always
have, and maybe, just maybe, always will. I also think my
feet are especially attractive. They're really not much different in appearance from when I was a girl. I think my face is
quite interesting and beautiful, and my thick, wavy brunette
hair is going gray very gracefully.

Now that I've done that cursory assessment, I feel the
need to show appreciation for my body, and this is where

celebration comes in. What a body! It has served—and continues to serve—me so well over all these years.

These feet and legs have taken me on thousands of hikes, walks, and strolls, up mountains, down hills, through parklands and parking lots. I am in awe of the ability of such relatively small feet to carry my body for so many miles. I feel gratitude every day that I am able to transport myself on my three-mile nature walk. It's my meditation time, my therapy, my spiritual renewal, and, twice a week, my "coffee klatch." I used to think of my knees as being knobby; now I think of them as two of my most treasured joints.

My hips are wide, and thank heavens for that. I was able to carry and deliver my twins without any problems. And these wonderful breasts produced enough milk to feed both of them for eight months. A fading scar on my right breast reminds me of the biopsy I had, and helps me to appreciate my breasts both inside and out.

Smiling at the mirror, I have to say, what fabulous teeth! And they're all mine. I can eat popcorn and crusty bread and chew gum. My eyes aren't 20/20 anymore, but with glasses I can see just fine and read to my heart's content.

The lines on my face show the results of laughing a lot. They reflect my nature and my character. Why would I ever want to pull my facial skin tight over my face and lose that history?

Body surfing is a great sport! And I'm gonna ride the crest of this wave right into my old age.

Getting Up There

                     ❧ CLAUDIA MORTON

She's up there in age, they say in the South
No spring chicken, they say out West
Past being a woman of a certain age, they say in academe
An annuitant, they say in Bureau-speak.

She's Joe's mother, Mark's aunt, Andy's great-aunt
Erika and Eli's step-grandmother
And step-great-grandmother to the children of
    Kathy's sons
Except we don't know where they are or if they are.

She's been married off and on for forty years
To the one she's always with
And ignored for the last twenty years by the one
    who fathered her son
(She surely missed the boat in picking men).

She was no more than a clerk for thirty-five years
At the university where she graduated
In ART, OF ALL THINGS

Just a plain, unfabled existence
Of a California woman getting up there in years.
The world is full of people like her
And you wonder why God made
So many of them.

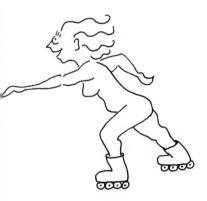

Viagra Blues

& ROSE SOLOMON

Ever since Viagra burst upon the graying scene with its
promise of erectile revival, I've been scrambling to find my
place in the New World Disorder. Pfizer Lab's claims *are*
correct: the bright blue pill delivers an erection that just
won't quit. It is more than a cure for impotence; it makes any
erection better. Now the young, blinded by the marathon
mentality of the super-fit, are using it recreationally, and
older men for whom the penis is the fountain of youth are
determined to be in the running. Just think, men will be boys
forever! But what are women to do?

In the rush to get the wonder drug, no one seemed to
care. Some women, including me, got caught up in the hype.
We watched our men join the stampede, hell-bent on hot sex
despite the warning label's dire list of possible side effects:
persistent headaches, sharp drops in blood pressure, heightened sensitivity to light, and blue vision. ("Not tonight, dear,
you have a headache.")

While India and Pakistan tested nuclear devices, men in
other parts of the globe tested Viagra. A Japanese travel
agency offered one-week Viagra trips to Hawaii, complete

with two bottles of Viagra to any man who submitted to a physical exam and blood tests. Italians created a gelato flavor called Viagra, even though it contains not a milligram of the substance. The whole world had turned on.

I boarded the Viagra bandwagon when my husband, Sam, brought home six samples that he'd bartered from a drug company rep who wanted the self-designed GET IT UP windsurfing T-shirt that Sam was wearing. We knew the turquoise, diamond-shaped pills retailed for nine dollars each. What a deal! Having an illicit stash made us feel heady and young.

Too many times history has passed us by. We graduated from college right before the student uprisings of the mid-sixties. I missed the Free Speech Movement at Berkeley because I was student teaching. With notorious bad timing, we got married before the sexual revolution took off. Now, at age fifty-six, Viagra offered a last ditch chance to correct our course and join the in-crowd.

Not knowing how such a potent pill would affect a still-functioning middle-aged penis, we decided to cut it in half—the pill that is. Since the instructions said it takes up to an hour to work, my pioneering guinea pig swallowed half a pill and returned to his desk. I got in bed with my *New Yorker* to wait.

In less than fifteen minutes my pioneer reappeared with a huge smile on his face and a tumescent appendage protruding from his pants.

"Already?" I asked.

"Looks like it," he said. We examined it. Our inspection

had a clinical quality, full of fascination but, for me, lacking in lust. Lackluster. Lustlacker. I envy the pride that the owner of an erection takes in its quick arousal.

"Look, it's gone from a soft soft-on to a hard soft-on to a soft hard-on just while I was sitting at my desk," said Sam. He was using the vocabulary invented by my cousin to calibrate erections. We agreed we'd better hurry and enjoy the hard hard-on that was soon to follow before it faded. This was the life cycle of erections as we knew them.

To me the most interesting thing about the erection was that it was progressing quite nicely without intervention. A touch here and there maybe, but it followed its own predestined course that filled me with the same wonder as watching a beautiful moonrise.

I set aside my *New Yorker* and dimmed the light. I settled back, committed in theory but unaroused in fact. This encounter felt mechanical and disembodied. Viagra might be a giant step forward for mankind, but a giant step backward for womankind. Were we reentering the Dark Ages of the Penocentric Pleistocene? Had attempts to civilize and broaden the sexual experience failed? After thirty-three years of marriage, I was suddenly back to square one, eyeball to eyeball with a show-off prick, which by now was standing at full attention, a hard hard-on. What a showy, inflated, self-absorbed thing! Something was terribly off, as if I were going to bed with a stranger, a mindless stud.

"I think I should take Viagra, too," I said, desperate to douse the unerotic rebellion that was welling up within me.

"Why?"

"Well, I don't feel ready," I said, not wanting to explain.

"You have an unfair advantage. Here, I'll take the other half."

I swallowed it and consulted the directions again. Pfizer made it clear that Viagra would enhance erectile function but said nothing about libido.

"Oh, dear," I laughed, "we're going to have to re-read *The Job of Sex,*" our favorite spoof on the subject. Beneath my joke lurked a distressing weariness that I am reluctant to confront. It's not that my libido has deserted me entirely, but that I don't miss it more. It's a relief to no longer live under its tyranny.

These days when I'm gardening or reading, I'm not interrupted by a sense of unease that (somewhere, everywhere?) couples are making mad, passionate love and here I am alone. If such a thought does surface, I'm happy to finish my solitary task, mildly annoyed to find myself falling into passive agreement with all those average Americans who rank gardening and reading as their most ardent pastimes on sex surveys.

Twenty minutes after taking the Viagra, my eyelids and nose had a sensation of swelling. The engorgement lasted several hours but unfortunately never spread to those heralded erogenous places. Nipples and clitoris would have slept soundly through it all if Sam hadn't awakened them with touch.

What followed was a hard-on marathon that made me yearn for the good old days when the dramatic life of an erection was clearly delineated. The mechanics of ejaculation used to signal the end of a sexual episode, and the demise of an erection resembled the curtain coming down after a magnificent act of grand opera. I knew when to applaud and shout

"Bravo" or "Encore." I knew when it was polite to get up and walk around, to talk about the performance or other things.

Instead, I shifted uneasily while *Homo erectus* showed no sign of leaving. Even Sam was confused. One half dose of Viagra had brought down his adaptation of Descartesian logic: "I shrink, therefore I am" no longer applied. Neither of us knew quite what to do. Was this a wet dream come true? Were we to go straight into the next act without a snack or bathroom break? Could this be the male answer to "I Could Have Danced All Night"? Not wanting to be a spoilsport, I tried to silence my thoughts, but they kept straying to those cautionary tales that warn us mortals to be careful what we wish for. Was a curse imbedded in this pharmaceutical blessing?

Sam later reported that a residual, half-mast erection lasted well into the next day. Using my cousin's scale, the hard hard-on fades to a hard soft-on and stays there, reminding its keeper that something has been left on, like an iron on a low setting.

I consulted Viagra chat rooms on the Internet to find out what the half-life of Viagra is, but no one could tell me. I eventually did find information about diehard erections in the *Physicians' Desk Reference*. It describes a "terminal half-life" of about four hours and warns that in the event of prolonged erection and priapism (painful erections longer than six hours in duration) "the patient should seek immediate medical assistance." I wonder how 911 response teams manage these emergencies?

Our home experiment with Viagra demonstrated that neither of us cares much about an unquenchable penis.

We're not enthralled by an iron rod with no capacity for nuance and improvisation. I'm glad we're not seventeen or twenty-four or even thirty-two. I like the vicissitudes of a middle-aged penis with its highs and lows and ups and downs. Vulnerability is an aid to intimacy, and unpredictability can be alluring, even funny. We can toss out the overwrought media images of what sex is supposed to be and enjoy some surprises. On the scale of human suffering, is a soft hard-on or no hard-on really such a terrible thing?

I used to be convinced that it's not an option to be unaroused or not interested. Afraid of being labeled frigid or asexual, I bought into the Freudian fixation on the penis as the be-all and end-all of sexual experience. From my perspective now, Freud's obsession seems pathologically self-serving. The great mystery of human sexuality is too supremely personal and varied to reveal its secrets so easily.

So what does this woman want? No strutting studs, please, or egomaniacs. Just give me a kind mensch with lively passions and an appreciation of the absurd, who's content with his paunch and mine, who's willing to listen and change course if necessary, and who will be there tomorrow and the day after, no matter what our anatomical or other highs and lows may be. I doubt that General Viagra with his simplistic mission, his global armies of erectly marching phalluses, and his growing arsenal of pharmaceutical weaponry is ever going to deliver that.

Old Snake

☘ SABINA SEDGEWICK

Old snake, soft at the core,
Coiled around myself.

Don't prod me with sticks.
Don't pry at my scales.
I'll bite.

Act ladylike, you scold.
Turn venom to apricot tea.
Old snakes can't afford
to be dangerous.

Old snake, soft at the core,
Questing tongue signals *come.*
Massage my spine
I'm not too old to shed my skin.

Lewd to the core,
Sliding out of my knot,
Cavorting nude on sizzling rocks
Lusting for new entanglement,
I'm hot.

156

Some Things Time Cannot Wither . . .

✑ CLAUDIA MORTON

We sit in the darkest corner behind a high mahogany bar, so dimly lit it could be night—although the afternoon sun slants through cracks in the wood shutters. He orders a "grey-hound," with a Chardonnay for me, but the drinks merely sit in front of us as our excuse for being there.

We haven't been together for so long. Where do we start? Luckily he's brought photos of a trip he just made back to his childhood home in the wartime South. The pictures show us a rural grace, a landscape and climate and pace of life so elemental that we who live in cities might be viewing a foreign country.

"Would you like to live there again?" I ask.

"No," he says. "The reason it's so luscious to look at is that the air holds water during the heat of the day and releases it in the cool of the evening, so that the sky weeps and everything sweats." He pauses, lowering his voice, "I'd rather sweat for other reasons."

His look is suddenly direct and brazen. We are both remembering other places and other times—superheated without the help of a hot climate.

⅋   ⅋   ⅋

We have a history formed by accident and family. We are distantly related, but with backgrounds in opposition, and we didn't meet until college. We were in love with other people then—quite a range of other people, as twenty-year-olds have the capacity to be. But we sometimes went out together in lulls between romances, or when we needed a date for social occasions that no one else quite fit.

Without our inviting it, a slow-moving sensuality developed between us. Time took a slower beat and our romantic ideals faded to black as we toured each other's young bodies in a state of delight. All the other connections, including our blood connection, melted in the forge of a physical attraction we could only wonder at. I felt a momentary guilt of incestuous pleasure that heightened the senses but receded in the sweet mingling of touch.

A fraternity beach party with steaks cooked over a campfire found us staying on after everyone else had gone—testing the sand as bedding and finding it unyielding without the sun's heat. Still the freshness of desire and the glow of coals warmed a lovely chamber for us in the black night.

At a sorority ball we danced a degree closer with each number, until he was sweltering in his tuxedo and envied my bare-shouldered gown, under which I wore almost nothing. We left early, retreating to his classic car to balance out our attire in the safety of its generous front seat. When his jacket and shirt were off and my high-heeled sandals had joined his formal black shoes on the floor, my tissue-weight blue gown was easily coaxed to my waist by his perfect hands, and my bouffant skirt provided full cover for our frolic behind the steering wheel.

☙ ☙ ☙

In time we both married other people—as was appropriate—and became even more different from each other than nature had made us from the start. To me, he was bluntly pragmatic and prejudiced; to him, I was mentally soft and pointlessly empathetic. We had never agreed on anything beyond the erotic impulse.

There were years when we were out of touch, yet when we randomly crossed paths the same heat wave of readiness arose. Then came episodes, unplanned, in which we leveled propriety to make it fit any terrain that presented itself. We knew that there was no excuse for what happened between us, only that, inevitably, it happened.

☙ ☙ ☙

Today, in a dark bar, we are together again briefly. As we talk, we laugh a lot. I've always liked his jokes, clean, clever, unlabored. He likes my anecdotes and I spin out the tale with which I am keeping him entertained, like Scheherazade postponing her termination.

Still, when our hands touch, they keep on touching. They take on a life of their own, his slipping under my light summer shirt and slowly traveling up to my breasts. Mine warming his knee, then working its way up his thigh.

"It's been a long time," he sighs, and we sigh it together. The young bartender cannot see our hands, but he can

159

see our gazes lingering and hear our voices dropping to a murmur. He moves to the other end of the bar to watch television. Old-age sexuality must seem ridiculous to him, or at least inappropriate. Besides, we are not buying the sequence of drinks that keep him in business.

"I think we're out of place here," I say, and my old paramour gives me a wry and tender smile.

"Where can we go, and when?" he asks.

Neither of us has a plan, but his touch becomes more intimate, his hand nestling into the tight crotch of my cotton pants, as if it had found a home there.

"You're making a slut of me," I say.

"The slut in you is what I like," he says.

He makes a proposal for immediate fulfillment at a nearby inn, then realizes his schedule won't allow it. I offer a postponement that I could possibly arrange for, but he couldn't.

Time moves back into its accustomed traces, the drinks finished, the bill paid, and we go out into the late afternoon light. I know his body so well I could diagram it, with his most sensual points highlighted. I think of his real kisses and his animal-like call at orgasm. As we say goodbye, I kiss him lightly on the lips and he draws back. We both sustain marriages, and his has succeeded while mine hasn't. He is suddenly shy, and we go our separate ways without a detour to the promised land.

🚲　🚲　🚲

At home I write him a haiku—which he'd never understand and, anyway, will never see:

> Let's not think that we
> Are old; time still stops for us
> As it always has.

IV. O Solo Mio

Oh the pain of it! Oh the joy of it! One Lady wants to be connected; another wants to be free. Of course, all of us would prefer to do the abandoning than to be abandoned. Who wouldn't? Yes, we agree that men leave. For business trips, for outdoor adventures, for other women, for evermore. And the children? Where are our children? They, too, have left. No matter.

At one time or another each of us has floundered, wandering dazed through the house, cooking, cleaning, rearranging, making beds, wondering if our former charges are eating well and remembering to fasten their seat belts. For who are we if not the caretakers?

With no one at home for us to fuss over, befuddlement and apprehension gradually give way to the vaguely guilty recognition that we are free. Free to travel now to places that we have always been curious about. Free, perhaps, to revisit old loves. Free to leave the door open, turn up the music past all reasonable decibels, and dance, dance, dance. We rediscover that onanism is something of an art and that pleasure is once again in our own hands. The cat leaps onto the bed, secure that it will be permitted to stay. The dog swaggers, knowing that it is the guardian of the house, the protector of its first lady. We cook rarely and eat randomly, comfort foods from an earlier time. A banana dipped in chocolate for breakfast. A three-course four-star lunch with a friend on the spur of the moment. An omelette for dinner. We paint our toenails orange. We fart unabashedly. Life is good.

The Bed's a Fine and Private Place

& CLAUDIA MORTON

The dark is gentle at my house—the ghosts have gone. Creaking ninety-five-year-old timbers no longer alarm me. I open my upstairs bedroom window to the smell of wood smoke and winter's approach. I have a huge bed with down pillows, soft old sheets, and silky mohair blankets that are almost weightless, and the bed is all mine. I can stretch my legs and arms to the furthest corners and just barely reach them.

I felt strange when I first started sleeping alone. So many years of sharing a bed had left an imprint on my unconscious that to sleep alone was bleak and scary. For many months I slept restlessly. A street conversation took place under my window with hostile overtones leading to—what? A vehicle roared through the stop signs at my intersection escaping— what? A cry from an animal—or was it human—signaled what? The freight trains highballing along Third Street, barely audible in the daytime, now sounded as if they were coming down my street. And fire sirens, if they went on very long, always brought me to the window.

My fire chief father had an announcer's speaker with a fire bell in our hallway, which called him to duty with a verbal message from the dispatcher, followed by the number of bells announcing the degree of the alarm. This told Dad whether he had to dress quickly and call his driver, or wait for a second report. Either way, the household could not go back to sleep, because the oilfield and dock fires of those years were extremely dangerous. If he did go, we worried the rest of the night. So I have become anxious for the men on red trucks roaring through the night—roused from heavy sleep to instantaneous action behind the banshee wail of the sirens.

But recently, less and less disturbs me, and even my dreams are more civilized—less concerned with being trapped in apparently benign places that, however, have no exit. I'm more likely to dream of sorting out some chaos or confusion— devoting myself to order—without much success.

۶ ۶ ۶

My bedroom windows face east, and before my eyes can perceive any morning light, the winged creatures do. In the fall, there may be a robin warming up with tentative chirps for his farewell concert before heading south with his family. The muted whistling sound made by doves' wings signal at any season the offering of coos to yet another dawn. Gradually the cold gray of first light becomes the rose-orange of a lightly clouded sky, and I'm amazed at a part of the day I never had the chance to admire before. Sunsets I've loved and watched avidly—anywhere in the world—all my life, but sunrises are new to me. They occur in the mystery zone of my biological patterns, where in my working years I was still fighting to stay asleep. That last bit of sleep was precious, because there was never enough. Now I know I can go back to sleep after I give sunrises their due—one more facet of the day to love for a non-morning person, followed by a rested, full awakening.

I put on some Vivaldi to accompany my coffee, since there is no one to argue my choice or make me change the volume. I linger over my newspaper. Maybe it's uninspired writing but it is print on paper-my favorite medium—which I choose over little lighted screens. There is peace, which slow-wakeners crave.

I feel like I'm floating on calm water, fresh to new knowledge. I take my time: my garden is untended, but it does not nag; my writing is unfinished, but it does not fidget. In time I'll have the dishes washed, the laundry underway, the shopping list drawn up.

No one instructs me and I find there is a balm in Gilead and a bliss in solitude.

About Face

❧ NELL PORT

It's warm and quiet, the lights are dim, the room
cave-like—and there's soft music playing. I hear trickling
water sound, and inhale the aroma of what's to come. I feel
myself stepping out of the mundane into another very faraway world—far from the cares and worries of everyday life.
I take off my clothes, change into a smock, and lie down on
the soft, clean, white sheets. Jessica covers me with flannel
and a warm blanket and puts pillows under all of my parts
that need pillows under them. Then she begins her magic.

The nurturing that comes through her hands makes me
drift blissfully back in time. First she cleans my face thor-
oughly, gently massaging in the cleansing lotion and then
wiping it away with warm, moist cloths. From then on, I just
lie back, close my eyes, and give myself over to her wonderful fingers and hands. She cleanses, masks, cleanses,
massages, caresses, and strokes while I drift in and out of
awareness and dozing. While the first mask does its work,
she massages my scalp, lulling me even deeper into semicon-
sciousness. During the second mask, it's my fingers, hands,
arms, and upper chest that get special attention. And some-

168

where in between, she does facial acupressure, which makes me feel cured of every possible affliction.

All my cares are gone. All the toxins in my body have seeped right out through my pores. I'm as relaxed as I've ever been. She asks if I'd like to have my brows tinted. Sure.

When she's all done, Jessica sprays the air above me and tiny droplets of scented water float down to where I lie. I remain there for a few last delicious moments, and then get up and get dressed.

I give my daughter a big, loving hug, thanking her for this wonderful gift and reminding her of the times long ago when I stroked and cleansed her sweet, soft baby skin.

I look in the mirror and smile at what I see—no makeup, but pure, unadulterated, clean and glowing me. And ooh, those eyebrows!

The Darker Season

Ω CLAUDIA MORTON

Now the fall sun glints the sugar crystals on my cafe table
Now the concrete sparkles random bits of quartz
Now the lone ant heads out businesslike and brusque
Now the sedges hunker down against their stony forts.

They say the year is dying with the light
They say the birds all know it's time to leave
They say the dry leaves rattle like the dead
And aspens quake the way that mourners grieve.

They say that crackling log and lighted lamp
Are all that save us from the madness of the dark
They say that ancient fears roust us from calm sleep
To warn us of the blight from winter's mark.

But now I'll walk out on my coastal heath
I'll find the trail I lost in summer mist
I'll find the lilies sprouting from debris
And mushrooms that the fox has missed.

Now I say I'll see the galaxy grow bright
And I'll hear the owl's lowest tones
I'll feel the earth's long sighing night
And bless this deepest quiet in my bones.

Beginning Again

✎ SUSAN HUTCHINSON

In my dream, a big pig was staring at me from across the massive dining room table. He rested his left forehoof on the arm of his huge, baronial chair, and with his right one shoveled food into his chops. He was wearing a natty, pin-striped business suit and a smug expression. I was a prisoner in his expensive, chilly seaside hunting lodge and was dressed in a thin, red-checked cotton shirt and cutoff shorts, but not permitted any shoes. Inexplicably, Pig allowed me one possession, my tennis racket. He fed and barely clothed me in exchange for sex.

I knew that I must, that I had to, escape; I watched for that moment when Pig's attention might be distracted long enough for me to flee. There were three exits. At my back, the door that opened onto the ocean was the easy escape. It would be quick and simple to rush out and drown. I rejected this. I could have marched boldly out the glass front door. But that was useless. He'd spot me instantly. Without shoes I couldn't run fast enough to escape. The last choice was the thorniest—to slip through the kitchen door and down the service alley, which was rocky, full of briars, and unkempt. It was hidden from his view and he would not expect a barefoot girl to choose it.

The moment came. A hallucinatory vision of luscious green fields on the far side of some forbidden fence briefly clouded Pig's sight, and he looked away. I grabbed the chance and dashed to the kitchen, through the outside door, and down the back path, ignoring my bruised and scratched feet and arms. The alley ended halfway to the far end of Pig's front lawn, still in sight of the dining room. To complete my escape I had to cross that open space without attracting Pig's attention, then bolt through his game forest to a distant hill of beckoning light. Beyond lay freedom—and hope. I mingled inconspicuously, ragged shorts and all, amongst Pig's elegant, self-absorbed guests who paid me no heed. The lawn stroll succeeded. Once into the woods I ran for dear life. Pig finally noticed my empty chair and sent his armed foresters out to recapture me. When I was almost close enough to touch my goal, a lone forester strode into sight. I was terrified and climbed a tree to hide. He immediately spotted my feet through the branches and pulled me to the ground. While he was stuffing me into a dirty gunnysack to drag me back to Pig, I begged him to listen to my story. The forester, having believed Pig to be an honorable employer, was shocked by it and offered to help me escape. He covered me with autumn leaves for camouflage and bid me lie motionless until Pig should lose interest and call off the hunt. I did. Pig eventually did. And I raced over the hill with my racket, which was my art, firmly gripped in my hand to whatever new mornings and life.

℧ ℧ ℧

I listened to the dream and let it guide me, despite the pull of a twenty-five-year marriage. The resulting divorce was devastating—and, oh!, the loneliness. New mornings of bright life felt as distant as the farthest galaxy. Until healed, I relied on a beginners' folk dance class—a class I joined because my best friend Marge was simply tired of watching me go through the motions of living like a listless ghost.

On that Monday evening, following another weepy dinner at my house, Marge said, "Tomorrow I am picking you up at 6:30. You *will* come folk dancing with me, so don't argue. Wear comfortable flat shoes, and *pretend* you're having fun. We learn the polka, czardas, waltz, tarantella, and many more. We do squares and every kind of line dance, including Chinese."

I really had no choice. I went along with Marge and hesitantly joined in the first no-partner-required line dance. Although I felt self-conscious and occasionally as if I had two left feet, I didn't have to pretend I was having fun. Moving rhythmically arm in arm in a line dance with an anonymous crowd felt exhilarating and was a release. I felt alive again.

At first, I sat in a corner during the couples' dances. But the second or third time. I attended class, one of the husbands, probably at his wife's instigation, asked me if I'd like to do a square with him. I told him I didn't know how, and he said he'd teach me. We twirled and skipped and clapped and do-si-doed. The dance was a rumpusy romp, but, not wanting to monopolize someone's husband, I retired to my corner after it ended. I did get back on the dance floor several more times during that evening, as a number of the unattached males asked me to dance.

I quickly realized that some men were better and much more enjoyable dancers, and I wondered how to attract them. As a girl from the forties and fifties, I'd flirted for attention, but these many decades and a marriage later I'd forgotten how. Heady perfumes or pretty new dance clothes were beyond my energy as yet. And I simply could not bring myself to initiate a dance invitation on my own. I couldn't go that much outside my dance upbringing dictums. In those ancient days, one could be either a wallflower or a chosen flower, no in-between.

Flapping eyelashes at a prospective partner felt false and a little silly—always had. But what about a bold, admiring stare? What would that do? Or a well-aimed glance over the shoulder while prancing a polka? Well I'll be danged—it lassoed me a pardner for the next square dance. I found the courage to approach another prospect, Mick by name, and begin a conversation with him about his handsome cowboy rig. That wasn't so difficult, and I'd found another person to dance with. When he complimented me on my footwork I was mortified to find myself lowering my eyes and looking up at him through my eyelashes—batting them, I believe it's called. He seemed utterly enchanted. I found that men were not necessarily rational—nor mind readers, for that matter.

It was the rule that men and women changed partners often—so as I became bolder. I had plenty of opportunity to practice my new "skill." There were Ned and Andy and Nate and Sim, and what was that last one's name? It was all so easy and comfortable and so informal. Before I married I loved any kind of dance. But inside marriage both dancing and flirting were off-limits. Now I began to realize that dancing itself was flirtation—and it felt so safe to stretch my wings inside the anonymity that the movement, the music, and my fellow enthusiasts provided.

I spotted a tall, gray-haired fellow with large feet and lots of bounce. Marge told me he was a physicist with a sense of humor and no wife. I wondered if I could get his attention. A friendly smile in the middle of a spin and I did.

And then there was Claude, the sweet retired structural engineer who grew up in the mountains of Washington and loved the freesia scent of my hand cream. I adored his touch with the waltz. I thought that I might even learn to like him outside the folk dance class. We found ourselves chatting between dances and after class—my art, his work on job sites in strange and glamorous settings all over the globe. He found art, which was so bread-and-butter common to me, exotic. I found his travels exciting. We became friends, and with him I temporarily forgot about playing flirt. When he missed a class I missed him—the feel of his strong hands around my waist, his sure lead on the dance floor, his kind and lovely smile.

I enjoyed my various partners, but they were, except for Claude, merely dance partners, and I assumed that was all I was to them. Flirting was fun in a make-believe world of dance, but not quite anything I felt like pursuing in the real world, where who knew to what perilous pitfalls it might lead—to something serious?

"Anyway," I thought, "I need a smidge more practice."

C is for Contentment: A Recipe

CLAUDIA MORTON

Under the C of Contentment, I cite Cows, Cream, Consolation, and Comfort, but I leave out Calories and Cholesterol. Through their milk, cows convey subliminal memories of infants sucking at the tender, engorged breasts of their mothers. Milk may be the origin of our human need for physical closeness, and cream in all its forms carries a hint of our first experience of that deepest comfort.

I encounter the direct gaze of the Guernsey cow nearest the split-rail fence where I stand, and I see a meditative curiosity in the wide, beautiful eyes. This huge creature, who could kill me by inadvertently stepping on me, instead supplies me with the wonderment of her creamy yield in so many forms.

Yogurt with a touch of dill, mixed with thinly sliced, lightly salted, and chilled cucumbers and sweet red onions can revive me better than a mint julep in hot weather.

In cold weather, a generous dollop of sour cream in hot borscht brings out both the sweetness of the beets and the sustenance of the broth. It could save me from hypothermia.

Ricotta, that bland, creamy filler of Italian crepes, is a chameleon. Whatever you give it for flavor, it absorbs and enhances. As a layer in lasagna or eggplant parmigiana it creates a touch of creamy difference. In a crepe seasoned with herbs, or with meat added, it becomes manicotti or cannelloni after being baked and dressed with marinara sauce. Blend ricotta with brown sugar, cinnamon, and cloves, and it becomes, baked in its crepe, a dessert perfectly paired with a glass of marsala. Add a spoonful of preserves and the crepe becomes heavenly.

Lately, I'm in love with a Middle Eastern version of our cream cheese called kefir. A touch more sour and slightly thinner, it can be stroked on a slice of smoked salmon and rolled in a thin cabbage leaf for a delectable hors d'oeuvre. A spoonful of kefir on a spicy tamale cools and richens. In mashed potatoes, a little goes a long way to decrease blandness.

Finally, there's Devonshire clotted cream, which Americans usually experience for the first time in southern England on a toasted scone with red currant jelly and perfect English tea. There are no clots in this thick, spreadable delight.

To make a dessert that celebrates the pure delight of creaminess, use the snowy simplicity of yogurt as a base and add some kefir to stiffen it or some sour cream to richen it. Shake in some powdered cloves and ground nutmeg, and add a pinch of salt. Dice and stir in some candied ginger or chopped pecans. Spoon a nice mound of this mix into the center of each dessert plate and surround it with fresh berries or ripe figs (peeled and quartered). When no fresh berries are available, canned poached baby pears are a juicy alternative. Sprinkle brown sugar lightly over each dish and serve with a sparkling Moscato wine.

I sing the praises of the creaminess that comes in cartons, jars, cups, and pots, and must be consumed without delay. Ephemeral joys are the most treasured.

Breaking Up Is Hard to Do

& NELL PORT

It happened in my fiftieth year: within two weeks of my daughters (ages twenty-one and twenty-three) both moving into their own apartments, my husband of twenty-nine years moved out. Two days later, the tile in my shower fell on my head, adding insult, as they say, to injury—not caused by the tile—which didn't help matters.

Although I knew our marriage wasn't perfect, I believed in its permanence. So I was shocked when he told me he needed to be on his own for a while to work out some of his issues. I couldn't understand why he couldn't do that while we were together, but he felt strongly that he could not.

Any woman who's had a similar experience knows the score—the anxiety, panic, and terror. The terrible pain of feeling alone, abandoned, rejected. Then the anger, the hate, the rage. The constant crying and inability to eat. One friend called me and, when I told her about the separation, asked how much weight I'd lost.

Who was this man I thought I knew and loved? I didn't feel that I knew him at all anymore. What I did know was that I needed to focus on my *self*. While I was aware of how important this was, it was also very painful.

There's no formula for how to cope with being alone, but several experiences that first year told me that in fact I wasn't alone and that I would be fine.

March. Santa Barbara: I dozed in the backseat of my car last weekend en route to a visit with Lucy. Marie and Doug talked lovingly in the front seat about lots of little things. It was a warm, wonderful sound, and I felt released of any responsibilities.

We came to the ocean and the camp where the two of them, who are studying American Sign Language, were about to spend a silent weekend, using only ASL to communicate. I dropped them off with their gear, and then was back on the road, with Joseph Campbell on tape to keep me company. His voice was gargly but good to listen to. I could tell how old, yet how lucid he was. I got chills as he talked and told stories about myths, heroes, goddesses, love, relationships, and sacrifice. He spoke often of finding what you love and following your bliss.

I was halfway through the six tapes just as I arrived at Lucy's driveway. She came out to greet me, and we picked up a conversation we must've dropped when we last talked.

We sat on her deck drinking apple juice, catching up with kids, work, her house being for sale. We went into Santa Barbara for dinner and the first of many long, intense talks about my life. The talk continued as we drove to her lover's house and slid into his hot tub. Lorne arrived, stripped, and joined us: the intimate, probing talk went on in the dark, so I couldn't see what he looked like, and it was almost like getting acquainted as a blind person. I instantly felt the love between them. I noticed the way he used her name, asked what she thought about something I'd just said, massaged her feet, and laughed easily with her. It made me happy to see Lucy so happy, and I longed for a lover like that. I felt warm and loved and loving one minute; empty and lonely and lost the next. My feelings were bouncing around uncontrollably.

Back at Lucy's, she built a fire and we polished our fingernails and toenails. Then the buried stuff came out and the tears started to flow. Lucy confronted me with so much: I need to nurture and love myself; I need to find my center, my soul; I need to push outside my comfort zone; I need to get off my "safety blanket"; I need to finally stop controlling myself, and when I do, the real me can emerge; I need to let go of the fear of being born into a new reality; I need to take some risks; I need to understand that living apart doesn't necessarily mean the end of the marriage. I need to go away to a spiritual retreat—Esalen; Tassajara; Ocamora, New Mexico; Findhorn, Scotland. I need to read poems by Denise Levertov. I began to feel more scared and confused. Why did I come here? But I knew why. Lucy knows me so well and is so honest. She was the person I needed just then. We hugged and I cried some more. I felt a little closer to knowing what I must do.

April. Berkeley: After a month of separation, I fell even deeper into disbelief, anger, intense pain, grief, terror, and rage. It feels so unfair. How could he do this to me? How could he throw away a marriage, a family, a home, friends, everything? What have I ever done to deserve this pain?

I stopped at Evie's last night and sobbed in her lap. It felt so good to have a friend just willing to be there—not to fix anything—just to let me have my tantrum.

The next day the kids came over. I felt so much love for and from them. They said I'll be fine. Alex cooked dinner and then we all went to see *Pretty Woman.* I was actually in a pretty good mood by bedtime.

The following morning I awoke feeling really down. I walked around and around the living room sobbing. Jessica and Marie held and comforted me. How could I let my kids hold me and comfort me? How could I not?

May. Movement class: Slowly I am finding that I can learn through my body. At the last class I began to see clearly that how I held my body, how I moved, sat, or stood, significantly affected how I felt. I could go from victim to take-charge person by uncaving my chest and moving with conviction.

> *As you believe, so you behave;*
> *As you behave, so you become;*
> *As you become, so becomes your world.*

It was almost like magic—for me it was magic because its newness allowed me to see it with a child's eyes. I focused hard on my own body and my need to concentrate on what I need, what I want, what I will do, who I am. In class I felt calm, focused, and good. I have much to do, much to learn about myself, many places to go, many people to meet. I was able to let go of some of my fear and start to experience excitement, exhilaration. I found myself looking for my "fire"—my energy, strength, vitality, youthfulness. I felt some of that fire in expressing and opening my body to the joy and warmth of my heart. I could let my anger and animosity go and was surprised at just how simple it was.

Yesterday I had a big insight: I am my own anchor. I can give up the fear of not having another person be my anchor. When someone else is your anchor, they hold you down.

June. Meditation: My June project was to transform Marie's old room into my meditation room. I draped the ceiling and put up billowy sheer curtains. I removed everything extraneous and added only my precious, special gifts from friends, including *A Room of One's Own,* a compass to find my way, a tiny wire and bead tree, a crystal, and a large ceramic egg. I found the perfect futon and put it at the perfect angle facing the window. I bought ceiling-high curly willow branches and put them around the room so it looked like a forest.

I learned how to quiet my mind and focus on my inner self. I will find out who is in there, what she wants and needs, where she wants to go, and whether by herself or with someone else.

July. Bolinas: I had a wonderful time watching the Fourth of July tug-of-war across the channel between Stinson Beach and Bolinas (Stinson won), a parade—the likes of which I'd never seen—eating lunch, taking a long walk on Agate Beach, a nap, dinner, and then fireworks.

Along with some very real feelings of "I'm going to be fine" and "I'll emerge a stronger, more whole person," I was still lying awake with the skin on my arms and chest charged with electricity. I've never understood what this feeling is. It scares me. The next morning I cried and cried—in fear and in sadness. Sadness—a deep, burning, tearing sadness at the loss of my mate, at the loss of innocent trust in the foreverness of that one person, the trust in loyalty and commitment. These are qualities I need so much and value so highly. Are they gone forever? Are they gone also for my daughters? I worry how this may affect their ability to trust.

I cried out because there was no one to take care of me anymore, and I still felt a need to be taken care of. Would I ever be able to take care of myself? I was feeling so all alone, and it terrified me. I knew I'd get through, but every time I moved ahead a bit, I moved back some too.

August. Santa Fe: Early July must have been the bottom of the pit, or maybe it was all the sunshine, but over the last few weeks, I've started feeling better and better each day.

Another grain of sand in my growing sense of who I am—a trip by myself to Santa Fe. There's a strong appeal in this high desert. The air, the mountains against the skyline, the openness, the clarity are all striking. The scenery on the high road to Taos was spectacular.

I am okay on my own. I can travel, I can take walks, I can go to dinner, museums, art galleries by myself or with friends. I don't need a husband to do this. I'm so proud of myself for treating me to a fabulous fiftieth birthday present— my own "Woman-in-the-Moon" ring. It's sterling silver, and the outer face opens up to an inner face carved out of ivory. It's beautiful. I'm a worthy person—yes!

Going home was scary though.

September. Portland with friends: The train ride to Portland through the Cascade mountains was magnificent. In Portland, trees, parks, fountains, and flowers were everywhere. It was clean and safe, and the architecture was varied and interesting. Next stop: Timberline Lodge on Mount Hood, people clomping around in ski boots. It started snowing at dinner and snowed all night and through breakfast. Beautiful and soft.

A spectacular ride through the Hood River Valley and the Columbia River Gorge. And a canopy bed—just for me!—at the Columbia Gorge Hotel.

Riding home on the train I felt as though I was on my way to my new life as the new me. It was frightening and exciting, but I began to believe what Evie told me—that I'd been given the gift of freedom. Only I'm just now feeling willing to take it.

# # #

There were many other turning points during that year: working out at a gym; psychotherapy; walking with friends; a "sisterhood" lunch; a trip to Esalen; a trip to Tassajara; starting hormone replacement therapy; getting a housemate; going on my first-ever backpacking trip (and loving it); going to my first-ever astrologer; taking a dance class; taking a drumming class; dating another man. And perhaps the most important factor of all was that I was earning my own money, and, as luck would have it, this was my most highly paid year ever. Because of my income boost, I had the luxury of a variety of activities, and I also had a feeling of power and self-reliance that wasn't there when I was dependent on my husband for money. It took all these experiences to get me to the point where I truly believed that not only could I survive, but also *thrive,* on my own.

During our year of living apart, there were many times when my husband and I turned to each other for advice, solace, and companionship. It helped me to cope at one level but could also be very difficult. At one point I felt a need to really become separate, and so we performed a formal separation ritual that Lucy wrote and sent to me. Not long after that, my husband asked if we could start seeing each other. I knew it was okay to embark on our new relationship. It felt very different from the old relationship, mostly because I felt like such a different person. One thing that hadn't changed was that deep down we still loved each other.

I think that my ability to focus on myself instead of on him, and my refusal to dwell on the negative, hateful thoughts and feelings that his leaving brought out in me, helped me to accept him back into my life. But I made him wait until I had a chance to explore another relationship.

Dating another man was quite a new feeling for me. The closest I can come to describing it is adolescence. I felt flirtatious and seductive. It was a lot of fun, but for the few months we saw each other, I felt this was a secondary relationship— that my primary relationship was with my husband—and this man sensed it too.

And so my husband and I dated for a while and had romantic trysts at his apartment. We talked a lot about what we had been through, how it had deepened us individually, and how it helped us both to clarify what we wanted out of our relationship. I grew to understand that what drove him to move out didn't have as much to do with me or our relationship, as it had to do with him and what he needed to find out about himself. I learned that his act took enormous courage and ultimately resulted in the strengthening of our selves as individuals, our relationship, and our marriage.

Psychologist Erik Erikson says that all long-married couples should spend a year apart. I know now why he said that.

We moved back in together fifteen months after we had separated, and shortly before our thirtieth anniversary. So we threw a party for our friends, which included a picnic on the grounds of the Berkeley Shakespeare Festival and an evening at the play *All's Well That Ends Well.*

Privately, I read my husband a marriage recommitment, which I renewed years later on our thirty-fifth wedding anniversary:

> I freely choose you to be my life partner. I learned that I can live without you. I don't need you in my life in order to be a complete, whole, happy, and fulfilled person, but I choose to be with you.

> I believe that within our relationship I am capable of growing, exploring, and learning about my own depth.

> I will not give up my self or my autonomy, but I willingly and lovingly agree to be mutually supportive. I will care for you sometimes and lean on you sometimes.

> I accept change in our marriage and in all areas of my life, although change doesn't come easy to me.

> I accept your imperfections. Your wonderful traits far outweigh them, and that's good enough for me.

BUT, I reserve the right to get mad as hell at you. I'm no longer afraid of my anger, and I'm glad you're not either.

Because I'm starting to assert my own wants and needs, we will have more conflict. I welcome it!

I enjoy being with you. I also enjoy doing things by myself or with other friends. I'm glad I can do all of these. And I really like having my own bathroom.

I've lived through "for better or for worse." I willingly renew these marriage vows with a strong commitment to the permanence of our relationship.

I cherish our history together, and I'm excited about our future together.

And now in our fortieth year of marriage, our relationship is more loving, affectionate, and respectful than ever before.

On cold nights, he turns on my electric blanket before I get into bed. Then he tells me that what he loves more than anything in the world is snuggling in bed with me. And not a night goes by without a good-night kiss and an 'I love you.'

In the morning, he turns to me, grins, and says, "Good morning," and gives me a big kiss on my forehead, eyes, nose, or whatever is peeking out of the covers. He goes out into many a frosty morning to get the newspaper.

He gives me fond, loving farewells when I go off to Calistoga or to Tuolumne Meadows with my girlfriends. He tells me I've never been more beautiful, even though I know I'm fatter, grayer, and wrinklier than ever.

He writes me birthday cards like this:

"And so my real gift to you is my true self. I value your

true self beyond measure, and I know you accept mine in the same heart-filled way. I love you."

And anniversary cards like this:

"Ours has been a dance of delight and struggle and the ordinary and the magnificent—just like us! I love you, need you, feel you constantly in my heart, which is the right place for us to be together—forever."

Some of my friends were lucky enough to find a new love when their old love ended. For some, this happened two, three, four times, or even more. I was luckier, I think, because I had a chance to find it the second time around with the same man.

Duo

⅋ SABINA SEDGEWICK

I'm on United Flight 161 from Chicago to San Francisco. The cursor of my laptop is blinking impatiently because I'm not feeding it with words. My eyes are on the cover of the flight magazine, *Horizon;* I recognize the steaming geyser and the swimming pool in Calistoga where we spent a night last year. This is a daylight shot, but the aqua color of the water cannot distract my vision of the two of us at midnight under a blanket of mist rising from the 100-degree water.

"The pool is open all night for guests," the receptionist had said, "but your cottage is far enough away to let you ladies sleep undisturbed." She smiled reassuringly. Disregarding the BATHING SUITS REQUIRED AT ALL TIMES sign, we ladies slip naked into the steaming water. All we can hear and see is the geyser burping white sulfur at the full moon. As we languidly swerve breast to breast, our nipples touch, our hands anchor at our favorite ports. In the green-gold shimmer from the underwater light our legs move side by side and intertwine like amorous aquarium fish.

In our cottage we don't bother stoking the fireplace. We fall asleep, holding each other tight, blotting out the year we've lived apart.

The captain has turned on the FASTEN SEAT BELT sign.
We will land in half an hour. My fingers are typing away to
fill up the screen. I try to look like Marsha Kerrigan, the
sober, sixty-year-old landscape architect that I am, but my
panties are wet. I can't turn off my desire for you, Isobel. It's
self-inflating like the oxygen mask above my head, which
will drop down automatically if the cabin pressure changes.
After we land I'm still on high sensual alert. I expect to see
your slender figure, wrapped in a wild-colored Guatemalan
sweater among the waving strangers at the arrival gate. I'm
waiting for that joyful leap inside my groin when you
emerge to greet me. "She's here, she's real. It's Isobel. She's
made it!"

But I walk briskly on, alone, to catch the puddle jumper
to Arcata. From my window seat I can see the four-lane freeway stretching north between miles and miles of dark green
forest until it shrinks to two lanes, twisting around redwood
groves and riverbeds.

As the little plane bounces along, I see the two of us
down there last year in the Bronco, loaded with sleeping
bags, butane lamps, and canned food.

"So where are we going?" I asked you. "To join up with
the Campfire Girls? Aren't we a bit old for making out in a
tent?

You grinned, "It's a surprise."

"Why couldn't we stay a few more days in Calistoga?" I
bitched. "I liked that pool. We should at least have tried a
mud bath."

So far I'd always done the research for our summer trips,
checking out the ads for a secluded beach or mountain inn.

The year before, while on a business trip, I'd reserved a fabulous hotel in Quebec. Still, I was intrigued by your unexpected e-mail: "Cancel hotel reservation for Quebec. New accommodations and transportation from San Francisco airport will be provided by Isobel on June 15."

I wondered why, after twenty years, we were meeting for the first time in your home state, California. I never really understood why you worried so much about running into some board member or teacher from your husband's school. But I accepted the fact that you had a high-profile life as a fund-raiser for the arts, and that you'd never told John about us. I thought, with John nearing retirement and your boys off in school, maybe you were ready to throw caution to the wind.

I never got up the nerve to ask you that question, so I'm adding another one—what made us cut out two weeks each year and paste them together? As if twenty years times two made up for the rest of our very different lives? Yours, with your family, your committees—commitments was your word—and I, with my sixty hours a week as a planner for urban parks, with some casual dates mixed in here and there. You'd let your hair go white since the previous summer, and I had put on ten extra pounds after quitting cigarettes. We joked about getting older. But in my mind you stay the same Isobel. In my mind, I string us together from summer to summer like a movie classic on video, where I can fast-forward or rewind my favorite scenes.

My little plane is dipping down to land in Arcata. I have a sweeping view of the coast and of timber stacked up like fortresses along the road, proclaiming the reign of the Pacific

Lumber Company. Then suddenly the amazing sight of hundreds of elk grazing in a meadow. I am replaying last year's trip again.

"Careful, they're wild," you warned, when I stopped the Bronco to take a photo of the elks. "The sign says you can't go over the fence."

"What's this?" I joked, "you're taking me to all these magic places with *verboten* signs?" I was referring to your damned rules, but you smiled happily, "Yes, that tells you we're in paradise."

Just as the Pacific Ocean turned indigo in the last reddish gold glow of the sun, you pointed the way to an unpaved road along the beach.

"The sign says no motorized vehicles allowed beyond this point," I cautioned. From what I could make out between the looming trees, the dirt road was rotted to the point that I could only hope to keep all four wheels on it.

"You want me to drive?" you teased me. I scoffed that I was used to the rough terrain in Chicago's asphalt jungle.

When you finally said "Stop," I was sure we were lost. But you hopped out, lifted the hatch, and said in that phony Girl-Scout voice, "Let's bring in the wood first. It gets chilly the minute the sun disappears."

Gradually my eyes got used to the absence of light, and I discerned a tiny log cabin in a grove of old-growth redwoods. You fiddled with a padlock and opened the rough-hewn door.

"Welcome to pioneer-land," you said, planting a kiss on my cheek before I could drop my armload of wood. A stone fireplace took up an entire wall of the one-room cabin.

"How come there isn't a NO TRESPASSING sign?"

"It's my cabin. My grandmother left it to me. She died two years ago. She was ninety-six. She used to bring us kids up here to play pioneer. Just when we were having the most fun, she'd tell us it was time to leave. That way we'd want to come back every summer, she said. John and I brought the boys here until they complained that there were no girls and no TV."

"And no shower or indoor plumbing?" I said after I had inspected the sleeping loft.

"We always used a copper bathtub. It's in the pantry, see?" You opened a closet, crammed with junk. "We'll clean it out and put it in front of the fireplace." When I failed to show my enthusiasm—you knew that I take at least two showers a day—you added another comfort kiss. "Wait until I've given you a sponge bath." Then you opened a blind closet in the log-paneled wall and took out a bottle of Jack Daniels with two tumblers.

"How's this for starters? I've also brought down sleeping bags. And for emergency bailout, there's a three-star AAA lodge at the end of the lagoon. If you row with the tide, it only takes twenty minutes to get there. A strong shore wind and you'll end up in Japan."

We couldn't have found a safer hideaway. So much for throwing caution to the wind, I thought. We finished the Jack Daniels and climbed into one sleeping bag, using the other for extra cover, together with a pile of musty-smelling blankets.

Later I woke up for my three A.M. pee and clambered, cursing, down the ladder from the loft and outside to the nearest tree. I was afraid an elk or bear might block my way to the outhouse. Hunkered down, I didn't feel cold at all, to my amazement. And when I looked up through the branches, the Milky Way seemed a lot brighter than Chicago's suburban streets. To say nothing about the air. The redwoods seemed to be breathing softly down on my head, and the stars kind of winked at me as if they could see what I was doing. A woman doesn't exactly look graceful in that pose.

What the hell, if this was some kind of test you were putting me through, I'd play lumberjack with you.

The next time I woke up, it was to the smell of bacon, and the sun was shining onto my face through the skylight above the bed. You had come up and were tempting me out of the sack with a piece of griddle cake. "I got the woodstove working, so there's plenty of water for us to bathe."

"Before or after we make love?"

I reached into the opening of your granny bathrobe, pink flannel. I hate pink, and I hate flannel. You knew that, of course. Your little tricks of pretend innocence matched the old-timer ambiance of the cabin. I grabbed your deliciously inviting thighs and pulled you on top of me. "Put your cold hands in here while I'm hot. Now tell me why is it that I keep adding those pounds every year that you shed? Look, I can circle your waist with my fingers."

"You think I'm too thin?"

"You think I'm too fat?"

"Let me see. Your breasts are fabulous. I guess your butt could use a little exercise…"

I shut your mouth with a kiss.

The next day you asked if I was fit enough for a three-mile hike to the public campground, which had hot showers.

"It's through Fern Canyon and then up over a ridge. It's virgin redwoods all the way."

I was familiar with the natural history of this forest, but I had never experienced nature's survival scheme firsthand. As we walked, just the two of us, like Hansel and Gretel among gigantic, primordial evergreens, you could have been introducing me to your favorite aunts and uncles. "They grow in family groups. I never feel I'm alone in these woods. Don't you get the impression they're watching us? Although to them we must look like banana slugs."

"Well, that leaves me out. Slugs reproduce like crazy. No wonder I buy my trees in pots."

"You're a pioneer, Marsha. The right kind. You grow trees where there's nothing left but concrete blight and rubble."

Moved by your compliment, I pulled you into my arms. I noticed that you were laboring to breathe. Your forehead glistened with perspiration. To impress you with my urban jogging fitness I'd been setting a brisk pace. So I asked, "How long have we been walking? Shouldn't we take a rest?"

You popped a pill into your mouth and washed it down with the last gulp from your water bottle. "For energy, low blood sugar, I'm okay." You went on with your stories about family picnics and games when you were a little girl. "Look, his trunk is burned out. We slept here one night, pretending we were Yurok Indians. You see that the top is green and healthy? Redwoods are great survivors. They've got scars from fires and floods. Do you know how many more years he could live?"

"*Sequoia sempervirens,* one of the oldest living things on Earth," I answered. "How do you know it's a he? Given the right environment, she'll be here for the next millennium, don't you think?"

"The big one in the middle is 1,500 years old."

"Pretty old for a virgin," I said. "Hanging on to your virginity extends your life for at least a thousand years."

You didn't laugh. I stopped beside a fallen giant, its roots tilted up above our heads. "Let's sit down," I insisted.

You shook your head. "She lost her footing, when the earth eroded around her roots. Now she feeds the bugs, eventually she turns to compost. Do you like that pronoun better, Marsha?"

I was worried. Your face had taken on the appearance of rice paper. "Maybe we should turn back."

"I hike this in less than two hours. We're almost there."

You refused to sit down until we came to a bench with a metal plaque: "Isobel Miller Babcock Memorial Grove."

"My grandmother." You accepted my water bottle and went on, "My great-grandfather Miller built the cabin in 1870 intending to start a lumber camp, but instead he opened a lumber mill farther north, where the trees could be floated down the Smith River to Crescent City. Grandmother gave the land to the park. She only kept a few acres around the cabin." You kicked up a pine cone with your boot. "I guess she thought I'd make it into my nineties like she did. She didn't know that I had leukemia."

My heart raced away from the words that pelted out of your mouth: "Remember back in '92 when I had to postpone our trip until spring? They did a marrow transplant and it went into remission. I felt fine after that. A new lease on life, I thought. Well, the lease is up."

"There are new drugs. I know a leukemia specialist..." I babbled on, afraid to let you speak.

"We're walking on layers of decayed trees, Mar. It's the soil for the new generation. You see the white skeleton tree up on the hill behind the creek? That's a ghost. Redwoods can stand upright years after they die. Sometimes I feel I'm already dead. I'm just pretending to stay alive. I wanted to wait to tell you all that, but it's too difficult. I can't hide my body from you, not from you, dear heart."

You had never called me that before. It sounded quaint, like something you'd picked up from your grandmother. It didn't fit me, I thought, but neither did my reproachful lament: "Why didn't you tell me? I thought we were friends. How could you keep something like—God—a marrow transplant?"

"When we are together, I feel really great. I wanted us to have fun. I wanted my escape to another planet. You are my planet, Marsha!"

"Then come with me. Stay with me. We can beat this thing together, you and I. Please, say yes. I really was going to ask you to live with me."

I kept on talking about how I envisioned my garden with the two of us arm in arm surrounded by flowering shrubs cascading from natural stones and rocks like those pictures in *Sunset* magazine. The caption would read, "Daring to live different."

You started to laugh. "You've no idea what you're suggesting. You're not a nurse. That's the last thing I'd want you to be, you silly-funny girl. But there is something you can do for me, something only you can do. And you must promise you'll do it."

You didn't tell me what, not until a day later.

A ranger drove us back to the cabin. He treated you like a top VIP. "The park people want the cabin for a museum. I've already willed it to the park, providing they'll bury my ashes under the big tree." I wanted to believe you were joking.

That night I bathed and cuddled you like a child. I experienced a confusion of feelings—anger, agony, anxiety, and tenderness. And shock. Suddenly your body no longer gave me that jolt. My fuse had no spark. Did I ever tell you that it was your shoulders that did it for me? I was mesmerized by your shoulders, when I first saw you at Smith. Just looking at your shoulders, when you walked ahead of me or when you opened the refrigerator—bang, I was hot. And now, suddenly nothing, except I'm aching with tenderness. I don't know what it's like to hold a child of my own, but that's what I thought, as I lathered your scalp with wildflower shampoo and saw my tears seeping into your soapy strands of hair. You turned around to splash my face. "I loved your hair, when you wore it long. You'd drape it around you like a veil."

"You don't like my haircut?"

"You don't like that I've gone white?" You splashed me some more, until I was soaking wet and I squeezed into the tub with you.

The next morning you wanted to go to the beach. "It's okay. I feel fine today," you said.

We took a gentle path to the top of the bluff. We stood with our arms around each other, watching the waves below churn and crash against the rocks. Instinctively I didn't let go when you stepped closer to the slick, muddy edge. "Push me," you said quite calmly as if it were the most normal thing to say. "Push me now!" And this time it was an order.

Clasping you tight, I yanked you away from the precipice. "You're crazy. You're mad. I'll stick to you like gum on a tennis shoe."

You started to laugh. I thought you'd snapped out of your suicidal mood. Then you went on, "I've got enough pills to kill myself twelve times over. I'm not going to die inch by inch, Mar, I won't go through this again. And I won't let John either. He'll take over. I don't want a coach. I've tried to go out with the boat. I've never been more alone. You've got to help me, please."

"I'll cure you," I promised grandiosely. "I'll be your doctor, your exorcist, whatever it takes."

"How about my lover, Mar? That's all I need."

Later I stoked the woodstove and put another log on the fire. I poured hot water into the tub and took off your sweats, bra, and panties. You lay in the bath with your eyes closed. I knelt down on the floor and started to rub your temples and forehead as gently as I could. I massaged your neck, circling my palms down the side of your ribs and up your spine to your shoulder blades. I felt the soft swelling around your rosebud nipples and the flutter of your little girl breasts inside my hands like baby birds. Scooping your buttocks out of the water I went on to kiss your stomach, your pubis, wherever you wanted me to go, as your breathing changed from sighs to gasps, "Oh yes, yes, don't go away." Spreading your knees wide I held your pelvis up and pressed my naked breast between your thighs.

We went on like this day and night, taking naps and

walks, eating when we felt hungry, randomly talking about anything but *it*. At night, under the oil lamp, you read poems to me from a tattered, leather-bound anthology you'd pulled from the log-mantle above the fireplace, *Sonnets from the Portuguese*, Victorian poems your grandmother had loved. You even tried some of the horrible recipes in the stained cookbook you'd found, using ancient staples like powdered milk and canned corned beef.

Your face regained its healthy color, your skin felt taut and resilient, your muscles firm. You looked once more like a girl. We are winning, I thought.

℥ ℥ ℥

I am sitting under the matriarch redwood tree in front of your cabin. Her trunk is as straight and strong as your spine. At the base is a shiny brass plaque with your name: Isobel Miller Babcock, 1938–1996." The ranger picked me up at the tiny airport and brought me here. He left me the key. He told me to stay as long as I want. I've brought my laptop with all my questions. I always do this with my clients. I make a list with all my questions. Once I get them answered, I can start to make a draft for my design.

This is a hellish thing you want me to do, Isobel. I'm not qualified to work out in nature. You knew that, of course. You must have made your bequest before you brought me here last summer. It's a hellish thing to be here without you. But then I have a strong feeling that you came with me on the plane. You are a most disconcerting and inappropriate ghost, Isobel—stubborn, too.

You did answer my questions, I think. Those two weeks we were together each summer were the fulcrum for us. Like a seesaw with your life on one side and mine on the other—our two weeks together were the balance. There will be a seesaw in front of the cabin. I'll use the most seductive piece of virgin redwood I can find. There will be a nature trail leading up from the campground to the children's museum. The ranger will tell stories by the fire and the children will play pioneer.

It took me a long time to find the courage to go into the cabin, Isobel. The copper tub is still in front of the fireplace. I can see you in the steaming water with your coltish legs hanging over the edge, saying, "I've never been happier in my life."

Missing Men

❧ BERNADETTE VAUGHAN

Here is the snapshot again. The print is faded, but the captured images are recognizable and heartstopping: the shimmering sand, the arching white sky, the incandescent ocean pouring itself over the horizon's rim, and a father, a little daughter, together on a beach.

Here is the little girl, mischievous and tousled in a skimpy playsuit. Delight is coiled in her small body like a silver spring. She crosses one bare foot nonchalantly over the other and leans in to him, smiling for the camera.

Here is the father, remote in his pale linen clothes, his Celtic fairness dazzling under the tropical sun, his hair a round halo, like a Giotto saint. He is courtly and fastidious. His gaze falls inward and his hand, holding the little fist, is flaccid at the end of a rigid arm; his countenance is guarded. He does not wish to be here, on this farflung beach, transfixed on the parental hook by this importunate five-year-old, his fifth, and as it turned out, last, child.

On the back, my mother's handwriting fixes the place and time: *La Plage de Hamm, Dakar, June 1940.*

❧ ❧ ❧

I am sitting at the dining room table, binoculars in one hand, watching a squadron of pelicans follow a school of fish across the lake. In my other hand I hold a pen, for I am addressing invitations to my son's wedding, which will take place across the country at the summer's end. He is ecstatic at the prospect of being married: he speaks of his happiness at being able to refer to his fiancée as his wife, of the beauty of the wedding rings they have bought for one another, of how ardently he looks forward to being a husband, a father.

He is the man I would die for. When he marries, I shall walk with him down the aisle, my left hand, heavily manacled to the corsage chosen by the wedding planner, on his arm. *I'll love you till the ocean / Is folded and hung up to dry....* I reflect on Auden's words, thinking how much more truthful it would be if, in these last moments of our life together, I were to carry a rose between my teeth. He would appreciate such a riotous antidote to the grim enduring tradition of the battle-ax mother-in-law. I have been feeling the need to inject levity into these solemn proceedings—not to mock the seriousness of the event or to diminish the intensity of the young couple's commitment, but to acknowledge the laughter, the radiance that my son has brought, since his babyhood, into my life. Still, I shall be calm. Composed. I shall watch him step away from me at the altar; I shall *give him away.* Can one really do that with love this vast? Fold it down to wallet size and tuck it away in a purse, behind driver's license and credit cards and snapshots of the grandchildren? There are no classes in this discipline; I am led to believe that it comes naturally. This, I suspect, is one of those self-perpetuating myths of parenthood, but it could be just another aspect of being a mother, a career that as far as I can see is accomplished on the fly from the great moment of birth until death us do part. So if all goes well, if I make it to my place in the pew and thence to the lectern to deliver the requested recitation of Sonnet CXVI (*Let me not to the marriage of true minds / Admit impediments*), we will embrace and—stupefied, bereft, but with mission successfully accomplished—I shall recede gracefully into my dowager's silenced shade. I shall be in his life, but as an onlooker. *A son is a son until he takes a wife.*

All of this will be recorded with cameras and none of it will include his father, for in my son's personal photograph album there are no snapshots of a little boy clasping his father's hand.

"These things happen," he says. "He blew it. Then his time ran out. We're left with that."

And so, as I sit here wondering if the bronze satin slippers I have ordered from that upscale catalog will indeed arrive in time for the wedding, the snapshot reappears. Here it is again, a survivor of the vicissitudes of time and travel and displacement, as renewable as skin. Unable simply to tear it up or consign it to cleansing flame, I have over the years scrutinized it with fresh astonishment, allowing new plays of light, new shadows, to develop on the hidden negative before it disappears again. I am not surprised to see it—although I thought I was looking in the old cigar box for the airmail stamps I bought to mail the invitations to England—but I am perturbed by its reappearance. I had tried to convince myself that the child, and the man, no longer existed; I had hoped that death and the passage of time would assert enough authority to ensure that their conjoined image would

recede. But here they are, a confutation of everything that
has ended.

I gaze out of the window at the glittering lake, at the pelicans serenely skimming the surface, their majestic wing beats
leaving the water miraculously unruffled. Time telescopes.
The shutter clicks, the flash of memory dazzles and begins to
burn, curling the corners of the old, shiny paper, and I am a
child again. I feel the vertiginous heat of the African sun, the
dead smoothness of sand-scoured shells; my nostrils prickle
with the odors of seaweed and of desiccated, white-eyed fish
and my own salty skin, then with my father's scent of pipe
tobacco, of smoke and violets and snowy, starched collars.
Then office smells of ink and carbon paper and old, peppery
dust. I see that the blinds that persist in my vocabulary as
persiennes are pulled shut against the afternoon's draining
light. I hear the slap of worn leather sandals, the scritch of
bare, calloused heels on floors strewn with wind-borne grit
and, beyond the jetty, the vertical, whooping blasts from nau-
tical funnels and the scraping, ironclad susurrus of anchor
chains plunging fathoms deep into the harbor's oily water. I
taste rusting metal and, my body reverted to its skinny child
form, stand once again on the stained steel decks of a cargo
vessel moored in the port. The marine accoutrements are
familiar, for my father, in some unclear but respected capacity,
oversees the delivery and distribution through French West
Africa of coal from the north of England. When a ship comes
in, he makes a point of taking his family on board to greet the
crew and take lunch with the captain.

It is a snapshot of a world that evaporated.

⚬ ⚬ ⚬

I pause, pen in hand, and watch the pelicans. I love these animated, cartoon petroglyphs. To me they are irrefutable indications that God's sense of humor was as rampant at the dawn of time as it has been at any time since. When they dive, they first rise in steep arcs; then, gawky and angular, they hang briefly outlined against the sky. One beat, two, and they start to fall out of the air, absurd constructions of beaks, wings, and great webbed feet, all cobbled together into an image of raucous ineptitude. I always hold my breath at the last moment: perhaps today I shall witness the first, unprecedented lapse of attention that culminates in a belly flop into the water, all that splendor and majesty exploding in a clownish, lethal pratfall.

That day on the beach, what were we pretending? Why was I—as sly, perspicacious, and complicit as a five-year-old can be—playing supporting actress to my father's dreaded starring role of *père de famille,* holding his hand, smiling, while my mother—French, shrewd and a realist—immortalized the moment with her camera? We all knew that my father, debonair and charming, erudite and musical, did not like children; we understood, my sisters and I, that we must not be naughty or rude or a nuisance, although, of course, we often and quite spectacularly were. Nonetheless, he presided over Sunday lunch (at which, surprisingly, my mother concurred with his edict that English must be spoken), monitoring table manners and banishing from the table whichever daughter murmured, *"That's not pudding, that's green slime,"* to her disgusted sibling neighbor. He paid for the expensive convent schooling, abroad and later in England, but he never involved himself; he never asked questions or helped with homework. He did scrutinize report cards at the end of term and congratulated the high marks, but he would not participate in other triumphs like the Christmas play or the carol concert, where, one year, I sang a solo.

Manners were important, and music and language and deportment. We were not permitted to use slang or, once settled back in England to endure the war, try on like dresses the rich regional dialect we heard in our daily exchanges with the village children. Once, at my mother's insistence—she never hesitated to invoke paternal power, even while simultaneously telegraphing her contempt of her husband—he made me write a hundred times the assertion *I am a blithering idiot* as punishment for what must have been a minor infraction, because, though spirited and curious, I was a very obedient little girl. And since for an attention-starved child, opprobrium always wins over disinterest, I was thrilled: for me those lines were a labor of love. My father's punishment put me on an equal footing with the children I chose as friends. I was the peer at last of those envied little girls whose fathers—so stalwart and potent that even with wartime shortages they somehow procured petrol for the cars that fetched their daughters from school—applauded solemnly at performances, cheered and clowned on Sports Day, and, with the jocular authority of male heads of households, teasingly interceded for them with the implacable, incense-perfumed nuns.

In Dakar, on the beach that day, was my father aware that the disease that would turn him into a gray-faced invalid for the remainder of my childhood had already taken root in his body? Certainly, he knew that his future, and therefore ours, was in a parlous state. I knew, too, because my sisters and I eavesdropped on my parents' quarrels and—*sotto voce* but employing the code that allowed us to pretend that things between them were better than we knew them to be— discussed what we learned. Escalating international tensions were eroding his England-based business. France had fallen, and the Vichy government—I knew what that was from my parents' explosive political discussions—was now in power. I assumed, and my sisters corroborated my assumption, that this was why the British colony, with brutal bureaucratic haste, had been told that it would be evacuated, against all survival odds, to Australia. My mother, glazed to brittle ceramic stillness with disbelief, had been given to understand that having become a British national by marriage she was now an enemy of her people and, what was for her immea- surably worse, under official pressure to terminate the preg- nancy that had only recently been announced to family and friends. (*"The voyage will be perilous, madame. A lady in your condition....We cannot be responsible."*) She was sure that the choice to join her husband and children in flight from a French colony would ensure her complicity in trea- son, while her acquiescence to an abortion was a sin against the Fifth Commandment. From my catechism class at the convent, I had learned that there is no forgiveness for such a transgression, only the prospect of eternal damnation.

Cracking under the strain, she erupted ever more frequently into the sulfurous volcanic rage that filled her household with dread. Domestic hostilities escalated to epic proportions. Now the neighbors in the apartment below regularly arrived to remove my sisters and me from the field of my parents' terrible battles. As regularly, they later returned us—such exquisitely dressed, exquisitely polite little girls, prettily curtseying our formal goodbyes (*"Au revoir monsieur, au revoir madame, merci pour vôtre hospitalité"*)— to the appalling, crockery-strewn wasteland onto which, after the screaming died down and the crashing subsided, the terrified servants crept from their hiding places to fatalistically restore order.

⳾ ⳾ ⳾

Some short months after that day on the beach, my parents packed such items of furniture and personal belongings as were permitted by the new wartime regulations. My mother stuffed currency and jewels into the hollow tummies of the rubber baby dolls my sisters and I played with tirelessly and enjoined us to carry them at all times in the days ahead. Weeping, I said goodbye to the beloved trio of servants: Camille, the nursemaid, Pierre, the houseboy, and Mamadou, the cook, all of whom had been such reliable bastions of love and courage, gaiety and succor in my world and whom I was forbidden to bring with me. As I sobbed and insisted, my father, embarrassed, looked helplessly around for my mother for God's sake to *explain to the child that there was a war on and even if there were not, dammit, darling, it's just not done.* We left the flat overlooking the shadowy, broad-leaved garden where the aborted baby, the forever perfect baby—my mother baptized him herself, she told me later, as the Church allows, in times of emergency, anyone to bestow the sacrament, and his name, she said, was

Michael—was buried in a tiny coffin under the black fig tree.

We boarded the tubby, doomed little collier, bound for Australia, that was anchored in Dakar Harbor, and my father withdrew to the captain's cabin to play bridge and drink brandy with the officers. After midnight, the pride of the French navy, the battleship *Richelieu,* was crippled at its moorings by the British. There was a brain-shattering explosion, the little vessel on which we slept reared like a terrified horse and keeled over, once to the right, once to the left; we were flung from our bunks. Water rushed past the portholes and our possessions fell upon us like hard rain.

The battle of Dakar, under the austere command of General de Gaulle himself, was under way. The demoralized British colony, hastily ferried back to land, now had to withstand the fury of the big guns as, from the direction of the sea, the town was bombarded. My father, along with the British consul and the rest of the Englishmen in the colony, was transported to the military barracks at the other end of town and held as a prisoner of war. The women and children were taken to a hotel and, to my immense satisfaction at such enhanced status, also declared prisoners of war. I experienced the sequence of events at a child's detached, observant remove, but I remember the heat of the room, thirst slaked by slivers of ice, the mattresses covering the windows to absorb flying glass, and my mother's hysterical tears. Later, transport was found and we rattled off through the bush at breakneck speed. Once in Sierra Leone, we joined a British merchant convoy and sailed through U-boat-patrolled, shark-swarming seas to England.

Throughout all this upheaval and uncertainty images of my father are vague. He is wraithlike, insubstantial, always evaporating. I turned my affections on the steward who made himself responsible for me in the event of torpedo attack: He laughed a lot and hugged me and reminded me to fetch my life belt, which was to be worn at all times, when I forgot it in the cabin; he stationed himself at my side during lifeboat drills and coaxed me to eat at mealtimes. He called me Max, the pet name favored by my father.

ஃ   ஃ   ஃ

Instants before they hit the water, the pelicans reveal comedy's dark source. They transform into spears. Shape, speed, intent become one: at the moment of impact, their bills pierce the placid water of the lake as if under orders to drill holes and drain the planet dry. Dropping dizzingly from past to present and back to past, I remember the only time I saw my parents touch. It was after my brother, my parents' firstborn, died in a plane crash at the end of the war, some eight months after his own daughter's birth. My maternal grandfather wrote from France, requesting with heartbreaking reticence details of the accident. He addressed the letter to my father, who read it aloud, translating the formal, exacting prose into English: *"If it is at all possible, my dear boy, be good enough to send me an account of the last moments of our beloved child."*

I saw that my mother's hand was tightly clasped in my father's as he read.

ஃ   ஃ   ஃ

Perhaps, that day on the beach all that long time ago, my parents, with nothing much left to lose except the shame they shared, celebrated a cease-fire. Perhaps, to my father, the prospect of changing into tennis whites and going to the club for a couple of matches, to be followed by cocktails and the lacquered, gossip-laden exchanges that colonials have always relied on to reassure their presence in the plundered land, was suddenly as acrid as the quinine we swallowed for the recurrent, bone-shaking malaria. Perhaps a vision of unbearable loss came to him that day: of the impending bankruptcy that was threatening his hard-won wealth and attendant social position; of his implacably advancing disease; of his vitality dwindling as his elegant, blue-veined right hand slowly lost its cunning and transformed into a shiny purple puffball, useless for months before his arm was amputated, the entire shoulder neatly sliced off like bacon in a delicatessen. Perhaps he came home instead and, full of sorrow, saw my mother standing in the apartment in a bloom of velvet light, dusky, scintillant, smelling of sandalwood and seaweed, a pulse ticking in her throat. And she looked up and met his gaze and they remembered an earlier time of flickering desire, so when he stretched out his hand and touched her breast and, circling her waist, drew her toward their bed, which was draped, like all our beds, with mist-white netting, she leaned against him and her heat rose. And then, later, perhaps they lay together, drenched and viscid, gleaming like kelp in the aqueous light, and searched each other with urgent lips and hands; and, as she arched into him, he looked into her huge wild eyes and saw that they were soft with the memory of love or forgiveness, and his own filled with tears.

And perhaps their passion drowned them so that they were unsure of anything but their need to end their war, to find peace at last within and beyond the reach of their fleeting embrace. And so, stranded, their hands at rest—his, white shells caught in the black sea wrack of her hair; hers, on his chest, brown starfish curled on a stretch of speckled sand— they slept. And when they awoke, the glowing grace of their aftermath, like the sun lowering on the horizon's rim, gave them both hope, a promise of redemption amid the fire, and, grateful but mistaken, they tried to give each other parts of themselves that should not, could not be given.

So they put the children in the car and drove to the beach and, with the ocean and the glittering sand as witnesses, they took photographs of what never was.

☼   ☼   ☼

Three years have passed and once again, I am watching the wonder-struck, midsummer sky, anticipating the return of the flinty avian fossils, the season's trenchant vaudevillians. I am looking at snapshots of my son holding his baby boy. This is the man he would die for. Long before he married, my son, whose vivid Gallic beauty reflects nothing of my father's sun-wary fairness, would speak of the children he wanted and would love unconditionally and never abandon. I see that covenant in the passionate connection he shares with his son. Here are angels, I think.

I go to the cigar box and withdraw the photo of my child self. I lay it, creased and faded, on the dining room table alongside the Kodak-bright images. I half-close my eyes and it seems to me that every moment leading up to that day on the ancient, blinding beach and afterward has been redesigned. Light, configuration, intention—all are rearranged, sweetening the long process of goodbye. The father, his face alight, bends over the little girl and points out the horizon and the magnificent, comical birds. The figures are posed in the landscapes of time and love and will, where broken patterns can be reassembled.

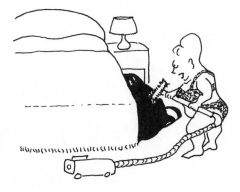

V. Ah, Men!

*"...Love is of man's life a thing apart.
'Tis woman's whole existence."*
—Lord Byron

How profoundly men influence our lives. In our formative years, we were shaped by the attentions and inattentions of fathers, uncles, brothers, and, later, by our choices of lovers, husbands, male friends. We nursed them, loved them, anticipated their needs, and indulged their foibles. Most of the Ladies have accommodated men in ways that stir amazement in our liberated daughters. For we grew up in a time when women were the emotional barometers in the home. One glance and we measured his fatigue, irritation, amusement, disappointment, hunger, contentment, boredom, or arousal. No emotion escaped our detection. Born into the roles of peacemaker and enabler, we spent a lifetime reacting to his moods and needs while often overlooking our own.

One great satisfaction the Ladies take in being older is looking back and discovering our own inextinguishable spark. In hindsight we see how often we caught the curveball that men threw our way, but sometimes there were setbacks that left us terrified, confused, devastated. In our stories a wife flees, a husband abandons his wife, a daughter comes to terms with her father's empty rhetoric, and a wife cushions her elderly husband's decline. We had no choice except to muddle on.

Other times, passion triumphed. A long-established couple hit the trip wire of attraction that united them in the first place, shocking themselves out of complacency. When we relaxed and let down our guard, past lovers reemerged from the mists of time and held us close.

Time has changed us and, without intending it, we are no longer adversaries: men have become our comfort, perhaps because we've learned to be easier on ourselves—and on them. Although men may remain unfathomable, we take delight in describing and analyzing them. We think and talk about them when they are not around. Our failure to change them makes us laugh now. We admit that we enjoy their voltage at every age—oh, how they light up a room!

Rude Awakening

✍ ELVIRA PEARSON

"What are you doing down there?" Not as provocative as it sounds—I had scooched down in the bed so that I could rest my head in the curve of his arm. Startled by the gruff tone of his voice, I quickly moved up until we were head to head, and I stayed there in a puzzled, tentative state, saying nothing but feeling that I had done something quite silly.

To my surprise, I had no sooner reached my full length on the bed when *he* scooched down and nestled his head in the curve of *my* arm. Our legs, as if on cue, slipped into a layered position where knees and thighs and calves managed to entwine themselves comfortably. Thrown off balance emotionally, I felt suddenly unsure of what to do. I aimlessly ran my fingers through his thick hair and, in a kind of "there, there, everything's going to be all right," slid my hand down his back and pulled him close to me. In minutes, he was breathing that quiet rhythmic sleep of contentment reserved for little children in the loving arms of mommy.

For my part, I was wide awake, trying to puzzle out what had just happened between my new lover and me, my thoughts spinning out in all directions as he slept peacefully in my arms. I was a bit surprised at myself for acting like a helpless young thing who wanted to be taken care of. Wasn't that what my nestling into his arms had suggested? Yet even as I stroked his head, I had to admit that I was really not comfortable being the "there-there" person. That was my sister's place, not mine.

My thoughts drifted back to childhood when my older sister looked out for me, showed me off to her classmates, played games with me when I was sick in bed, and taught me all the combinations of x plus y equals z long before I needed them in school. And hadn't it been she who plucked out my first loose baby tooth? I can still hear her saying, "It's just like picking a flower," as she waited patiently for me to overcome my terror. "Can I look?" she finally asked. I opened my mouth and, in the next second, she was proudly displaying my tiny tooth between her thumb and a forefinger not much bigger than mine.

The more I reflected on it, the more I wanted to shake him awake and tell him in no uncertain terms that *I* am the one who gets taken care of, not the one who takes care; that it had been that way from childhood, and he was not to think for a minute that I would or could change. Instead, as I listened to his breathing (somewhat like the noise of a teakettle as the water comes to a boil), I went on rummaging through my past for more evidence of my newly identified flip-flop behavior, which alternately had me brave enough to leave home at seventeen and frightened enough to then seek out people I could lean on—mostly men. To hold it all together took some sass and bravado, without which, I see looking back, I would have sunk into—I don't know what. Like many others in those circumstances, I didn't take good care of myself. I didn't eat much and I smoked, stayed out late, and burned the candle at both ends. With little money, few marketable skills, and no friends or family nearby, I could have been one of the runaways I read about every day in the newspaper. Whether these lost souls are escaping their middle-class homes or lives of poverty and neglect, I find my impulse is always to turn the page.

Fortunately, the men I met in my adopted city, 3,000 miles away from home, would take me out to the best restaurants, where I would order prime rib and Yorkshire pudding (for dinner) or eggs over easy, bacon, and stacks of pancakes (for breakfast). The ones who stayed around for more than a date or two must have seen me as needy, for they would invariably offer to fix whatever was broken in my life—a chair, a toaster, my record player—and they would pitch in to help when I decided to paint the rented rooms and apartments I occupied one after another.

The men, the food, the apartments all passed in a blur. I know now that I was lucky to find men who wanted to take care of me, yet, rather stereotypically, I found them to be "too good" and I treated most rather shabbily. Well of course I gradually changed and became more self-sufficient and certainly more kind, but, as was becoming absurdly clear to me in the small hours of the night, lying next to my lover, I never was nor will be the sort of woman who assumes that her inescapable mission in life is to take care of others. My meandering confrontations of self finally wound down and I dozed off.

As our relationship progressed, I began to realize that what had taken place in bed that night did not have all the meanings I had been busily attaching to it. We managed to accommodate each other as the days and weeks went by: I made him tea when he was tired and he rolled out the heavy debris can when I was tired. Little by little, I found myself relinquishing the *I'm the darling baby sister so take care of me* role that I had worn like skin for more than a half century. Curling up with each other in exactly the same way every night, his head cradled against me, our gnarly limbs entangled like the red rose and the briar, became a ritual I looked forward to.

Still, I sometimes wonder what might have become of us if, at that critical moment when he scooched down to nestle into my arms, I had thought to say, *"What are you doing down there?"*

Vigor Mortis

⇛ ROSE SOLOMON

Years ago I took up bodywork to cure Sam's bad back.
Not that he wanted me to. Sam is a balding action hero, who
gravitates to high-intensity sports whatever the cost. I watch
with growing alarm as he accelerates into a state of sublime
denial, bordering on delirium, that blinds him to bodily
harm. Years of immersion while windsurfing in the frigid
waters of San Francisco Bay and while flyfishing knee-deep
in icy Sierra streams have deadened his nerve endings. He
seems not to notice when a toenail falls off or a toe gets
crushed by a rock. He cannot account for the hematomas on
his shins or for the violent bruises on his thighs and hips. He
watches blisters on his palms turn into bottomless craters
with the same wonder that a religious zealot might view the
onset of stigmata. Only an occasional broken rib, again of
unknown origin, ever slows him down. He claims it's never
his sports that hurt his back. The culprit is usually a sock
lying in wait on the floor or a long ride in the car.

Still, it hurts me to see him hobbling about like a mangled
wire hanger, one hip and shoulder higher than the other, his
spine frozen in an asymmetric S. I want to change him
through osmosis, but the healing benefits of my own yoga

and Pilates practices never rub off. I try to cajole him into believing that some preventive maintenance will at least protect him from further injury, but when I entreat him to join me on the floor for a soothing spine stretch, he insists, "No, that's boring. It hurts. I hate it."

Sam's aversion to self-maintenance programs goes deeper than boredom. I think he resists them because they reek of mortality, reminding him of the limitations of the flesh and its impending decay. Which is exactly what I want him to face. My biological clock isn't just ticking. It is on wake-up mode. This is our countdown to eternity! Though we may be as doomed as the tiny ant tottering under its daily burdens, our dedication to an exercise regimen becomes death-defying and heroic precisely because of its futility. We should be getting ready for the last long march. We need to tone up our thighs, clear out the clutter, and pack our bags for the hereafter, but Sam won't hear of it. I am being overly punctual, as usual, and he is too busy packing his duffel for the next camping trip.

Who *is* this man I married thirty-five years ago, the one I was so eager to accept as my alter ego and soul mate? He is more of a boy now than he was then. I used to try to keep up, assuming that was what all good wives did, but a moment of truth on a ski slope four years into our marriage disabused me of that notion. We were skiing at the aptly named Heavenly Valley with a friend who, like Sam, was an expert skier. The two men were riding the chair ahead of mine to the top of the lift. By the time I disembarked, they were nowhere in sight. I didn't know if they had skied over to the Nevada side of the mountain or if they were still in California.

I decided to stay in California where the runs were familiar, but for the next few hours I skied with my head screwed on backward, scanning the mountain behind me for a sign of them. Finally, I gave up and skied on my own. Late that afternoon as I was coming down a narrow trail through the woods, someone had the audacity to swoop in front of me and screech to a stop with a showy spray of snow. When I saw that the smiling someone was Sam, I went berserk, shouted every obscenity I had ever known, and beat him over the head and shoulders with my pole. He shielded his head with his arms and absorbed the blows. Finally, when the pole had bent and my arms were about to drop off, I became aware of a muffled disturbance behind me. I turned around to discover that I was blocking the trail. A dozen amused skiers were stalled there, watching the scene and applauding.

That classic confrontation taught me that the man whom I'd regarded as my alter ego was, in certain contexts, a totally detached stranger. When he is skiing, he loves the sport more than he loves me. In fact, he is not even thinking about me. I have been replaced, and he couldn't be more elated. Similarly, when he is wave jumping on his sailboard, he is Icarus, soaring higher and higher on the updrafts of mania, away from me.

And it is not just skiing and windsurfing. When Sam returns muddy and bruised from fishing trips with the guys, I often ask what they talked about. He looks at me blankly and says, "What do you mean? Fishing."

"That's all? Not wives, not girlfriends, not kids, not work, not anything?"

"No, we were fishing."

Then we laugh, remembering the priceless scene in Robert

Altman's *Shortcuts* in which a bunch of day fishermen ignore
the presence of a submerged female corpse in the stream
exactly where they are fishing. Very late that same night, one
of the returning fishermen mentions the strange occurrence as
he climbs into bed beside his dozing wife. She bolts awake
and says, "You saw *what?*"—exposing in one brilliant
moment the full polarity of their priorities and sensibilities.

Much as Sam and I see ourselves in that couple, I cling to
a fading hope that the passing years will smooth away our
edges and make us more alike-or, better yet, make him more
like me. Instead, semiretirement has freed Sam to play all the
harder and to abuse his body every day of the week. It is a
constant bombardment. For the first year of his liberation,
he behaved like a fugitive, running from one escape to the
next. He fly-fished in almost every Western state, including
Alaska. Our dog Meeker and I, who tire of restless travel,
accompanied him on some of the summer trips, but when the
season changed, we hunkered down at home to work and
resume comforting routines.

Sam went off without us to ski and to fish in the rain. He
windsurfed for the month of January in Baja and for a week
in May with his buddies in Hawaii. Friends began to inquire
after him with thinly disguised irritation, "So where is Sam
off to this week?" There was an edge to their curiosity.
Enough was enough. Some wondered what he was running
from. "Me," I'd say. Others surmised that he was in denial.
"Yes, of course," I'd agree, for never had Sam been less
inclined to contemplate the future nor more insistent that he
was having the most fun of us all. When our scattered but
still vigilant adult kids commented on their father's manic

euphoria and nudged me to speak up, I told them I was giving him a year's grace.

Our social life with other couples shrank, and I had a very faint foretaste of widowhood. With Sam away for increasingly longer intervals, I found I could handle the days better than the nights. I made more evening plans than I normally do. I went to movies and dinners and concerts with friends. I especially chose plays and recitals that he would have hated. The longer Sam was gone, the more I took pleasure in the disciplined rhythm of my life. I cooked good meals for myself and ate them while reading my favorite columnists. I dined regularly with Tom Friedman, Paul Krugman, Anthony Lewis, and Frank Rich, conversing with them in my head. They were all the male company I needed, except for late at night when the house grew bigger and emptier. Without Sam, our king-sized bed didn't feel right, so I heaped piles of books on his side to simulate his reassuring bulk.

Aside from the clutter on the bed, I became uncharacteristically neat for a short time. I swept all of Sam's loose change, keys, notes, and candied ginger off the dresser top and dumped them on the desk in his study. I rearranged his clothes in their designated drawers and filled a box in the garage with items to be discarded. Last, I invaded his basement lair, tossed out junk, organized the tools, and vacuumed. Meeker, our working dog with a penchant for physical labor, approved. When there was nothing left to straighten, Meeker crawled onto the couch, and I tried to settle down at my desk.

My allotted work space suddenly seemed too small. Now

with all of Sam's projects out of the way, mine spilled over and usurped any free surface. Three years' accumulation of photos in search of albums spread out over the floor of his study. Tax preparation materials marched the whole length of the hall. Two unfinished book manuscripts covered the guest beds. Folders of editing swamped the floor of my study. Unanswered correspondence littered the bedroom floor, and a mountain of intended reading rose beside my side of the bed. Stepping back to survey the damage, I felt close to triumphant that my mess could take up so much space. What a self-congratulatory pig I could be! One by one, as these projects came under control, bare floors and surfaces reappeared, which gave me some feeling of progress.

Sam's dramatic goings and comings jarred my egocentric routine. There was a prickly adjustment at either end of his trips. His uncontained excitement over leave-taking stirred up my apprehension. He never tired of going, and, no matter how often he told me he wanted me to come along, I always felt that he was abandoning me. I could not understand why our life in Berkeley was not as compelling for him as it was for me. Was he really falling for Circe, personified by the nomadic sporting life with its carefree, no-strings-attached camaraderie? Should I not be tagging along, trying to woo him back?

Sam's absences made me examine what kind of wife I was. I refused to become his oppressive keeper, the albatross guard-wife who would monitor his actions and measure out his moments of liberty by the teaspoonful. Neither could I bear to remain the willing accommodator that I had been throughout the productive years of his career and our child raising. I was changing, too, in unintended ways, so that when I scrutinized the outward harmony of some of our longest-married friends' lives, I felt almost like a defector. I saw capable women whose lives revolved around a husband. They counted out his vitamins in the morning, cooked meals to his liking in the evening, and went to bed when he did whether they were in the mood or not. They performed his errands, ran the house, attended to his parents, and traveled everywhere their husbands wanted to go. Compared to them, I was sinking into criminal negligence. I wanted to go my own way and have Sam live with us (Meeker and me), on my terms. He wanted me with him on his. Neither of us was ready to budge.

Sam always did come home when he promised, but I didn't greet him with the fanfare due a conquering hero. He hadn't been at war or even at work. He'd just been at play, and I welcomed him back cautiously, reserving judgment. Sam behaved like a new tenant trying to make a good impression, as if he were home on approval. He accompanied me to family and social events. Though he was a model of cheerful compliance, I saw no sign that deep down he was really changing. Rather than "getting it out of his system," his year of adventure was setting a precedent, a baseline from which to launch more ambitious itineraries. I'd overhear him on the phone arranging repeat trips and adding new ones for the year to come. Like a pied piper, he was attracting a growing roster of followers, old and young, clamoring to follow him to the next never-never land.

During one of Sam's homestays, I overheard my mother quizzing him about where he was going next.

"You live like a person who has but six months left to live," she said.

"Of course," said Sam. "That's it exactly. Who knows how much time is left?"

Their exchange stunned me because it made me realize that I did marry someone who lives every day as if it might be his last. Sam is not in denial at all. Each day is a living protest against our terminal condition. On some level, I have always known this because from the start Sam's intensity has been my fodder for caricature, my source of sketches and verses over the years. He is my favorite cartoon character brought to life, and he enjoys playing that role to the hilt. For instance, when he returned from his second January in Baja, Sam appeared as a blue-footed booby. He clomped over the threshold wearing stiff, blue diving fins and carrying a latticed piece of cactus skeleton in his mouth. There, in the front hall, he did a clumsy mating dance before gently dropping the stick at my feet. Like the discriminating female booby ready to mate, I haughtily picked it up and accepted him back.

I did not notice until later that my blue-footed booby was injured. He had severed a ligament in one knee. The agility that he had always taken for granted must be earned now, and Sam has been hard at work on a rehab program under a physical therapist's supervision. Our bedroom looks like a cross between a gym and an S and M chamber with pulleys, weights, ropes, and balls rolling around. He's having to confront his own mortality without my guidance and is more afraid than ever that each day might be his last. New projects abound, and I don't try to straighten the Spanish language workbooks and tapes, the upgraded computer software and photography equipment, the folders of correspondence and half-written articles that clutter his study. The mess he generates reassures me that he is more than a mindless jock. I want him to go kicking and screaming to the grave with as much might as he resists my ministrations.

Around each other so much, we witness and chronicle our respective warning signs of senility. To date the score is almost even: for every faucet he leaves dripping, I leave on a burner. And when we're trying to get to a dinner party and he runs back into the house for the third time for something he's forgotten, I hold my tongue because I remember that last week I'd forgotten I'd driven to a local market and walked home without the car. He later retrieved it for me without further humiliation.

We are arc-crossed lovers on our separate ways to a common destiny. I plod on each day, groping toward self-preservation like a wizening Methusela fated to outlast friends and family. He flares like a meteor, emblazoned by its own willful self-destruction. He knows that if he dies before me, I will kill him.

The Date

&ℯ SUSAN HUTCHINSON

I was emerging from several terrifying years. Doing battle with cancer, heart disease, a torn shoulder ligament, and a back injury had made me feel as though all the joy and light and fun of romance had forever deserted me. It was my seventy-first birthday, and my partner had arranged a surprise. He was so taken with his plan, he wouldn't even give me a hint. Remembering some of his other surprises over our eighteen years together, I was filled with unease and foreboding. There was the glider trip over the Pacific Ocean; the helicopter ride *under* the Golden Gate Bridge; the commuter-plane ride, during which, to my horror, our untrained, eleven-year-old grandson flew and landed unassisted; the introduction to kayaking that upended us; and our first and last dirt bike expedition, which left me with a two-year-long back injury. I am too old to accept the possibility of breaking my parts. They take too long to mend.

Yet how could I spoil my partner's joy in a new adventure? I tried to hint around the surprise. What should I wear, blue jeans or something dressier? I was informed that blue jeans wouldn't do. Well, what would? That was up to me. Hoping for dinner, possibly at a really elegant restaurant, I did a major hair fuss and put on my prettiest summer dress.

At five o'clock he turned up saying, "Maybe you should wear something warmer," and I was tempted to crown him with a mallet. He saw my expression and hurriedly added, "Just bring along a thick sweater." Baffled—and ruffled—I did as he instructed.

Instead of heading out of town or toward any of Berkeley's usual "gourmet ghetto" destinations, he drove us to pretty Lake Merritt in Oakland. A bird sanctuary, it offers some rowboats, a large boathouse, and not much else to recommend it beyond reflections of the city lights at night. I knew it had no place to dine, and I'd always considered it strictly blue-jean territory. Years before I'd done a portrait of an owl there, but didn't consider the prospect of renewing that bird's acquaintance a major thrill. I could not imagine what my co-celebrant had in mind, and looking at the cold, muddy water, wasn't sure I wanted to know.

Nevertheless, he gallantly handed me out of the car and with a flourish produced a bottle of chilled champagne. Then out from the boathouse office stepped a crisp, blue-jeaned hostess. She smiled and said, "Your gondola is waiting. Our gondolier is in fine voice tonight." She and my date both laughed when I stood absolutely speechless.

We were introduced to our gondolier, Morgan. He was tall, dark, Welsh, and wore a red beret instead of the traditional Venetian straw hat. But in true Italian manner, he escorted us to our real, made-in-Venice gondola.

The craft was shiny new and beautifully constructed. It had velvet cushions and lap robes and an ornate double-chair for us (plus an extra small one up front for the duenna!).

With yet another ceremonious gesture, Morgan whipped out a tray of quasi-Italian antipasto and two champagne glasses.

Once our gondola began to glide, we lay back against the luxurious velvet and sipped champagne. The sidewise undulations of the boat nudged us together. I couldn't resist gently nibbling my marvelous date's ear, and we leaned cheek-to-cheek. In a floating, dreamy warmth, I felt his hand cover mine, then stroke my arm. I nudged his sandal off with my bare toe and tickled his foot. For an instant he looked startled, and I changed to caressing his foot with mine—between his toes, around his toes, over his arch, around his ankle. He gave me a wicked wink as I tenderly wound my fingers through his curling, snow-white whiskers. I giggled. He sighed. We stroked each other—feet, hands, faces. Feeling blissful—and faintly giddy with champagne—I toasted the balmy evening. He toasted our happiness. As the wavelets softly lip-lapped the sides of our boat, I snuggled closer into his warm embrace and gave him a long, long kiss.

Our gondolier gazed away into the distance and broke into fine Italian song. He paid our cuddling no attention, though some of the nesting cormorants looked slightly askance. He rowed us around the lake to "O Sole Mio," "Santa Lucia," "Ritorno a' Sorrento," and other ancient chestnuts. Then he switched to his own romantic favorites, 1930s and '40s American pop-love melodies straight out of his passengers' teens. His light tenor voice was pleasant and true.

Between sighs, sips of champagne, and stolen caresses we complimented him. He told us that on days when all three gondoliers were on the water caroling together, they created a true operatic performance. His contract supposedly limited him to only a few songs per boat trip, but we were having such a lovely time and he was apparently enjoying his unlikely elderly crew so much that he stretched his song limit all the way around Lake Merritt and back.

When our time was over, Morgan glided us back to the dock. As we passed within touching distance of the now sleeping and indifferent bird population, we shared one last kiss and watched the mellow sunset—pearl pink and slumbrous lavender.

Living Viagriously

      & ELVIRA PEARSON

God knows we weren't exactly young. I was in my early forties, he was in his mid-fifties. We had both been married and divorced, and we both had children. And yet, when we started seeing each other steadily, I felt and acted very much like a young girl in the grip of first love.

Our pattern was to go to dinner and a movie and, afterward, to his apartment—unless he was tired or not in the mood, two states of being that I, oddly enough, seldom shared with him. I spent the entire evening looking forward to being ravished by him at the end of our date. I tossed off his occasional complaints about "feeling old," words he always used in a sexual context, as natterings—"full of sound and fury, signifying nothing." From my perspective, sex was good—no, it was grand and glorious. The pungent smell of patchouli oil inhabited my nostrils throughout the following day and stirred up flashes of remembered pleasures from the night before. As he used to say, "Even when it's bad, it's good." And so, it was hard for me to understand the "feeling old" story he seemed so insistent on telling me.

In those early days, the way I knew whether he was in the mood or not was never because he said so: it was embedded in the ritual that took place when we were driving home. I remember it well. I would hold my breath until we came to the critical intersection that would tell me whether it was to be his apartment (lovemaking) or my house (goodnight). If he turned on the left signal it meant his place, the right signal, mine. As if I were sixteen instead of forty-something, the right signal felt like a rejection every time.

I regarded myself at that time, as did others, women and men both, as independent and outspoken. Yet, looking back, I am shocked at how compliant I was with this man whom I unabashedly thought of as my one true love.

We have now been together a good many years and we no longer speak of ourselves as an "older" couple; we *are* an older couple. Paradoxically, I suddenly find myself right back where I was, when older was much younger. No longer at the mercy of turn signals, now it is a diamond-shaped blue-green pill that he cuts in half an hour or so before he wants it to take effect, always needlessly nervous that it won't work its magic. The little cylindrical pill bottle that sits quietly in the medicine cabinet has assumed enormous power over our lives. He loves me, yes, but his *wanting* me has dimmed; his wanting any woman, it seems, has dimmed. I know that saddens him and makes him apprehensive about us, about what lies ahead. "Everything is different," he says. "You can't imagine."

I understand and I don't understand at the same time. If it is different for me, it is not different in the same way. I don't need to ingest a pill to assure a lusty response to his silken hand on my breast, his lips on my lips, his warm breath mixing with mine, and I don't need to plan ahead to be sure I am ready. On the other hand, I remember well when all of that cold preparation *was* solely up to me—when I had to make sure that my pearly plastic case housing my diaphragm, and a tube of spermicidal jelly, were in my bag. Then it was I who slid away an hour before to ready myself. Ironically, here I am now, postmenopausal and free of the need for all of that oppressive paraphernalia, ready at any moment to move into serious earth-shattering sex, and once again we are at odds.

Throughout the years, we have remained somewhat shy with each other around sexual matters, and, in that arena, we share a preference for subtlety that keeps us from saying much about what we want or like, even to ourselves. That sexual spontaneity is a thing of the past is something painful to comment on, and so we don't. Just as we don't throw caution to the winds and ourselves on the sofa, or roll onto the floor to start undoing buttons and zippers—arms and legs flailing, clothes flying—in those frantic moments before rapture carries us to a place where death itself is held at bay, at least for those few awesome seconds when the world stops.

Faced with this turnabout in our relationship, I sometimes find myself looking for clues throughout our evenings together, clues that suggest he might "want" me a bit later. But they are not as straightforward as they were years ago when all I had to do was wait for the left or right turn signal. Now I spin out a litany of silent questions: Has he been especially affectionate this evening? Do the pill bottles appear to have been disturbed? Did he look at his watch mid-evening and jump up to go to the bathroom? Has it been x number of days since last time? The one time I need not pay attention to the presence or absence of signals is when he drinks a glass of wine. A liquid red flag, we both know that the V-pill and alcohol do not mix.

Although the high drama of sex is gone now—meaning for one thing that I can finally find humor in my anticipation of directional signals that say, "Tonight's the night"—I sometimes wish he would remember that even when it's bad, it's good.

Frothing Forth: A Recipe for Rejuvenation

✍ ROSE SOLOMON

Whipping up a perfect latte is my man's Holy Grail. His is an elusive, contemporary quest that is won, fleetingly, only after prolonged effort. Once mastered, it becomes a measure of masculine prowess, envied by other men, particularly middle-aged men, and seen as supremely chivalrous by women like me who secretly long to be served. Even the most independent of hearts melts when a man on bended knee asks, "Caf or Decaf? With nonfat, low, or whole?"

Young men do not understand this. In their rush for instant gratification, they dash off to Peet's or Starbucks for an over-the-counter quickie in a disposable paper cup. In their minds, "courtly" means paying for their lady's take-out order. Many another promising suitor falls for pricey machinery. He thinks the result can be bought. Even worse, he assumes that he is doing his lady a favor by presenting her with an expensive chrome trophy so that she can make latte for *him*, a most unromantic role reversal.

I admire the red-blooded man who can produce a hearty froth with minimal equipment. When my Knight-of-the-Froth took up the gauntlet, fellow experts rushed to his aid. They buoyed his spirits with tales of their own strug-

gles. Our friend George, a dentist, confessed that nothing
in his long years of professional training had been more
arduous than the six months of trial and error he'd put into
perfecting the foam alone. Finding the right brew was
another obstacle entirely, as fickle and subjective as finding
the right wife—one neither too bitter nor too bland, but
robust and full-bodied enough to interest one upon awakening each day.

Jack, a Master of Espresso, paid a house call. Jack exem-
plifies frugality: no waste, no excess, just pure expertise. He
and my beloved bent over our array of mismatched equipment, their balding heads almost touching as they fumbled
in their pockets for reading glasses. With the precision of a
jeweler, Jack unclogged the spout of a milk steamer, then
filled the base with water, tightened the lid, closed the valve,
and set it on a burner over a high flame.

Next, Jack showed his apprentice how to use a salvaged
Italian stovetop espresso pot. This method is the reverse of a
drip system: water is heated to boil in the bottom section,
then flows upward through a fine sieve holding the coffee
grounds, and farther up into a pitcher-shaped top, where it
collects, fully brewed.

Jack ground only enough beans to make two tablespoons
of fine powder, which he tamped loosely into the sieve. After
filling the base with water, he screwed the parts together and
set the pot over the lowest possible flame.

"Leave the lid up," he said. "That way you can see when
the coffee starts to come." Like expectant tourists awaiting
Old Faithful, the men hovered close. Soon a brown liquid
began to ooze up to the top.

"Let it collect slowly, and turn off the heat the second it stops coming," said Jack. "It mustn't burn."

Then he turned his attention to the steamer, which was beginning to throb in an excited boil. Just before meltdown, Jack turned off the flame, took the steamer from the stove, inserted its long wand into a small pitcher of milk, and slowly opened the valve. A slow, steady sigh of steam gyrated through the liquid. With no roaring or hissing, only a low groan, the milk doubled, then tripled in volume. It rose to the rim of the pitcher where it stood as white and glistening as Mount Shasta.

A hush of shared amazement settled over the kitchen. The men beamed like victorious warriors. They had done it! Once more they had beaten back old age and decrepitude.

Was it good for me, too? Yes, indeed. I have taken to lying in bed on Sunday mornings, listening for sounds that presage a froth. A ping-ping-ping tells me that a wire whisk is whipping the milk in a saucepan over low heat. A whirring drone hints of a Braun electric mixing wand. Soon I will hear his careful footsteps coming to the bedroom, carrying his frothy treasure to me while it's still hot.

Reunited

– ELVIRA PEARSON

Dearest...

Do you remember the poem? "Now I love you and you love me," it began. You sent it to me years before, knowing those words would touch me—reassure me—that I was not alone in loving and wanting you as I'd loved no one before or since we stopped caring. Was it *we*? It felt like you who stopped caring, but now, so many years later, you say (surprising me with your vehemence), *"It was both. You withdrew and I withdrew, I withdrew and you withdrew."* No, I think to myself. Men withdraw. But no matter.

Having found each other again, we are thrown into a strange land. By some miracle, I re-entered your life and said hello, and you said hello, and suddenly we were holding each other tightly, warding off the coldness of age and death, stealthily advancing. (*"Don't look back. Something may be gaining on you."* Satchel Paige knew.) Of course we talk about the past. How could we not? (*"Let the past go,"* the daughter says. *"That was then. This is now."* Her intensity betrays her: she speaks her truth, not mine.)

We stand at the end of our lives retracing faded footsteps, daring to fantasize a future that plunges us into life and love

243

once more, but this time with promises that go beyond a need to reawaken dormant lust. Now we speak of "safe havens," of ever-afters, of—dare we say?—constancy and devotion. We speak fast and move quickly. There is so little time. (The daughters fail to see that.)

The quietly numbing flesh speaks more loudly to you than it does to me. I breathe life into you, you say. *"Yes, I will; I can,"* I say. You curl into the warmth of me and I feel my body swell and go large, my flesh white hot, as I envelop you, entangling my legs in yours, burrowing my hands into your hair, and moving your head to a safe valley between my breasts. Never the earth mother, I find in myself an unexpected tenderness as I hold you closer than close. In the next minute, caught up in your illusions, I turn long, lithe, slender, becoming the wild thing that dances naked in your memory. A woman of fire and quick movement. Unpredictable, playful. How I yearn to hear you moan with pleasure.

Who are these two women? I ask myself. I, too, am older, if not old. And newly shy. Unlike you, I easily relinquish the wild one from that faraway time for the one who is slow, sensual, loving, tender. You mourn—oh, how you mourn— your loss of power, of prowess, of potency. You *wanted* the wild one then; you *need* the wild one now. Like a man who has come home to find that the hill he climbed so easily as a child has become a mountain, you say to me, "You don't understand. It's nothing like it used to be."

Will you cling mindlessly to those years when you had no need to question the lust that hovered just beneath the surface of your life, ready at any second to be awakened? Reaching back into memories of our days together, I recall that ornery twist in your nature that made you scowl and pointedly look away when the "shes" of the world dared reach for you across a room, down a narrow aisle, on a moving train.

Surely, you knew even then that "she" was everywhere, waiting for you, ready, smiling her open invitation, yours for the asking. (I hear you protest.) Whenever you chose to, you could have returned her look with your own and electrified the air between you: *"Yes, yes, yes—come find me."* (The gentle woman side of you exulted in being the "found object.") I hear your barely audible *"Do me,"* as you fantasize her smoothing away your shyness with her hands, her mouth, her mischievous, knowing tongue. If part of you feared she might suck you dry, you would manage for an instant to forget that women will do that. *"Suck me dry,"* I hear you say softly, smiling that boyish smile I remember so well, as your hands lose themselves in her hair, then draw her waiting mouth down the length of your body. You hold your breath in anticipation. ...

I force myself back into the present. *That was then; this is now.*

In my life once more but still cities apart, you come and you go. For a time, I am alone again. I walk past all the pretty little houses of my pretty little town and find you "gentle on my mind." I come to the retirement home, where a gardener pushes his weight against his machine, letting the freshly cut grass fly back into its sturdy canvas bag. The sweet pungent smell fills my nostrils and I nod to him. He smiles. His ears are covered with Mickey Mouse pads against the noise, but he knows I am in love. *"Good morning,"* I say. I could have mouthed the words and he would have known. I could have shouted "I love you" over the blaring sound that locked us into that moment, and he would have smiled as he now smiles, and continued to push his mowing machine as if it were spring instead of fall, and as if he knew that I was crazy in love—and mad with hope.

To the Soft Fall

Ș CLAUDIA MORTON

When a relationship has been calm,
Unquestioning and full of pleasure,
What goodbye do you say?

When there has been no quarrel,
No rift, no resentment,
What ends a man and woman together?

She could say: I am forever wrapped in your life;
I could tell your story
As fluently as my own.

He could say: I cannot forget you
No matter how my life changes
With unforeseen destinations.

When silence gathers and no blame accrues
And there is nothing to mourn,
How do you mark a conclusion?

Where there never was a plan,
There is no betrayal of the plan.
Sadness hovers but does not descend.

A new era is evolving for both,
Without tears or a declared finale,
Or yearning for times past.

It does not mean that there was
No importance to it, only that there
Was no drama when it ended.

If it ended? That question struggles
Like a moth flying blind in a white mist.

Cook a Turkey, Be a Man

⅋ ROSE SOLOMON

The more deaf and blind my father gets, the more fero-
ciously he cooks. He cooks only meat, and he likes to do it
alone. In his culinary ardor, Dad becomes what he cooks: On
his eightieth birthday I watched him scuttle around the
kitchen like a lobster, boiled red, eyes bulging. On the Fourth
of July he splashed about the barbecue, as silver and battle-
scarred as the king salmon he was basting, swatting me out of
his way with long-handled tongs. But today it is Thanksgiv-
ing morning, and he is definitely a bird, beady-eyed and
beak-nosed, his head bobbing with every movement, his scalp
pink as a buzzard's beneath his transparent white hair. He has
consented to show me how he does it, so long as I remain
seated on a kitchen stool out of his way.

"Women don't understand meat," he bellows. "Not lamb,
not beef, not chicken, and especially not turkey. Never have.
You can't trust a woman to do it right."

He's been up most of the night, bathing the turkey in a
tub of warm water.

"She buys frozen turkey," he mutters. "The fool, the
goddamn fool."

He soars out of reach, high on his own bombast. I could form piercing words, take aim, and blast him out of the sky like the wild ducks he used to bring home from his father's club when I was a child. They tumbled, warm, damp, and limp, from the burlap sack onto the garage floor. I arranged them by sex: the splendid males in one row, their drab mates in another. The drying blood smelled sweet, turned sticky black.

Dad plucked and gutted the birds himself. He chopped off the mallards' emerald heads and the sprigs' gray feet, proclaiming these the best eating, then widgeon, then teal. He was a terrible shot, he said, hated that part of it, and left the killing to others. He made a point of keeping the gun at the club.

"Too bad you weren't born a boy," he'd often say. "Terrible to be a girl."

"Why?" I asked once.

"Because women have to be passive. You can't do a thing, no matter how smart you are. It's a waste. You should have been a boy, and Gar with his shyness should have been a girl."

Dad's pronouncement clouded my youth like a verdict and brought me closer to my brother, Gar. So, we were both defective in his eyes. It didn't occur to me then that he might be wrong.

Now at the kitchen counter, Dad dries the inside of the turkey carcass with a special chamois, "not paper towels, they leave lint."

"Sniff it," he says, dangling the naked turkey in front of my face. Its bony bottom smells of herbs.

"Mmmm, poultry seasoning?" I ask.

"God, no! Nothing prepared. I pick and pulverize sage,

rosemary, marjoram, chervil, and summer savory fresh from the garden."

He puts the turkey back in its roasting pan and wipes his hands on his stained khakis. He massages more olive oil into the puckered folds of turkey skin. "These poor legs," he says, fondling a drumstick in each hand. "They get so dry. Look, I made them leggings." He holds up a pair of cutoff cotton socks. "You don't want the dark meat to cook too fast."

"Nice."

"Better than nice. Brilliant. I'm goddamn brilliant."

What power his words once had for me. At the airport as I was boarding the plane for college, he said, "Don't turn into a Radcliffe man." With no time to ask what he meant, I marched to my window seat, half expecting to sprout chest hair and a beard. The fright and confusion unleashed by Dad's bizarre warning echoed an earlier scene with a boyfriend who'd huffed, "Just because you got into a fancy school doesn't mean you're any smarter than I am." Clearly, it wasn't right or natural for a woman to be smart. The many bad jokes about ugly 'Cliffies cautioned me to keep such a terrible disfigurement as a sharp mind well hidden, or I would be forever undesirable and unloved. By the time my plane landed in Boston, my sense of self had gone the way of lost baggage.

One of the first events of freshman week required all new female students to line up for the P.E. department's naked posture pictures, front and profile. I fell into place as mute and obedient as the others. We could have been lining up for a firing line, so meek were we. No one questioned this practice, even though we knew the pictures were stored in a vault

251

in the athletic department, which Harvard men routinely raided. Dad's words reverberated in my ears, "Don't turn into a Radcliffe man." I kept quiet in class, afraid that my voice might change if I used it too much. Before winter ended, as if responding to a post-hypnotic suggestion, my blood stopped flowing. My periods vanished until I transferred to Berkeley two years later.

The bright California sunlight made it easier for me to dismiss Dad's warning, but my tongue still could not form words to argue, with him or any other man. By the time I'd begun to find my own voice, Dad was growing deaf and couldn't have heard me even if he'd wanted to.

Dad struts to the stove to taste the giblet gravy.

"The best! I'm the best!" He clucks. He spoons the stuffing into the cavity, puffing himself up as he recites the ingredients: chestnuts, celery, onion, Italian sausage, sage, parsley, corn bread.

"Don't rush a bird or question a man," he says. "Never ask where he's been. Men don't like it, and you don't want to know."

From my stool in the middle of the kitchen, I suppress the urge to strangle him. How can someone of intellect be so hurtful, so unenlightened? I pretend to be an anthropologist, silently observing the last remnant of a doomed, chauvinistic culture. What kind of a Neanderthal is this? Just as I am thinking, "When he dies, I won't miss a thing except the chestnut stuffing," he lifts the turkey, tin cradle and all, and waltzes in dainty circles around me. He closes his eyes and whistles through his teeth a reedy rendition of Sousa's "The Stars and Stripes Forever."

The first time he ever sang it to me, I was playing in the bathtub, age three. He danced a mock soft-shoe on the white tile floor and sang, "Be kind to your fine feathered friends." He wanted me to admire his new navy whites before he shipped out to Okinawa. As an officer on a supply ship, he got to keep house for the men who had to fight and die.

These days Dad cooks for his dying brother. In a doomed two-year effort to get Bobby to gain weight, Dad keeps plying him with codfish balls, a childhood favorite. After one especially triumphant lunch, he phoned to crow that Bobby had eaten a pound and a half of codfish balls. "Imagine that," he repeated, "a pound and a half of food at one sitting!"

Now Dad's whistling "Rock-a-Bye Baby." I am not sure when the melody changed, but it occurs to me during this pause in his babble that I still long to love him. Perhaps with a different soundtrack, we could have conversed. Dad always says, "Do as I say, not as I do." But at this moment in his kitchen kingdom, stripped of the plumage of youth, the pomp of war, and the blare of his bluster, it's the reverse: do as he does, not as he says.

He tucks the turkey more snugly into its pan. He straightens the socks around the drumsticks and pats a blanket of buttered cheesecloth gently over the breasts. His fragile sweetness silences me as much as his loud harangues ever did, and I don't make a peep.

Twilight of the Gods

BERNADETTE VAUGHAN

In her sixties now, she is twenty-five years their junior but, to the old doctors, still the exotic prize carried off, amid scandal and consternation, two decades ago by their married colleague. Then, rising tentatively above the shock and dislocation of their small professional world, she represented slightly suspect renewal; to a cynical few, the triumph of hope over experience. But time has passed and all is forgiven; now she is ensconced in their affections, and their wives no longer view her as a menace. She leans in to them at dinner parties, wives on her right, husbands on her left, gives grave attention to the same stories she has heard and heard before, receives once more the same advice and facts, laughs at the same threadbare medical school jokes, and with tenderness and dread, accepts their elderly, flowery gallantries.

Tonight, she has invited them over, the doctors and their wives, to watch the Academy Awards. Vibrant and solicitous, she is in full hostess cry. She pours wine, offers cushions, discusses a William Grimes food column in the *New York Times,* critiques the Repertory's latest production, enthuses over the most recent best-selling P. D. James mystery. Silently, she wishes she had reconsidered her decision to serve dinner from trays balanced on the knees. She realizes that although the plan was practical, given the time of the television transmission and how long it takes the husbands to butter a roll, let alone absorb a three-course meal, this was not a wise choice. With the screen as the focus of garrulous attention, mishaps are inevitable.

"That's Helen Hayes. She got an Oscar for *The Piano.*"

"No, it's not. It's the other one."

"Oh, yeah, right. Helen Hunter."

"I don't remember this scene in *The Piano.*"

"It's not *The Piano.* It's the other one."

"*Man Bites Dog.*"

"No. *Man Wags Dog.* Good title."

"Holly Hunt was in that? Whaddyaknow."

"I don't remember this scene, either."

"It's all her different movies."

"Whose?"

"Hers. The one in *Man Bites Dog.*"

"You mean *The Piano?*"

"I didn't see a scene from *The Piano.*"

She watches the wives, perched beside their men, alert as birds on a wire, ready to fly to the rescue, to swoop for the toppling wineglass or the spilled sauce, to recollect, to prompt, to exercise their rank as repositories for domestic, social, and historical minutiae.

"Sweetie, watch your plate. It's sliding into your lap."

"It's called a *montage*, honey. Different scenes from different movies. They're doing a retrospective."

"Your sleeve, sweetheart. You've got your sleeve in the salsa."

"It's *Wag the Dog*, honey. The movie is called *Wag the Dog*. Anne Heche."

"Oops! Oh-oh. Oh well, darling. Here's a napkin."

They are exhausted, the wives, desperate for respite from the constant, debilitating vigilance. It was not supposed to be like this. Back when they were brides, hysterical with relief that the carnage in Europe had spared their husbands, they had been led to expect rewards for their constancy. They were so grateful, so loving, that the thorny irony couched beneath the euphoria eluded them. They did not notice that although the men were liberators returning triumphant, they, the women, had still to declare their own war of liberation.

So, banished from their wartime jobs and ordered home, the women stripped off their various uniforms and abandoned the nicotine-fueled bonhomie of factories, hospitals, and barracks for the kitchen's labor-saving devices. They tied on coy aprons and flew about the house in high heels and coiffed hair brandishing cocktail shakers, pushing the newest Hoover model, ecstatic over fragrant piles of laundry and recipes for macaroni salad and onion dip. They bore babies, put their trust in Betty Crocker, spent long hours under hair dryers, and submitted gracefully to the corseted, reactionary dictates of Dior's New Look. They slipped into splintered, girlish isolation, growing rivalrous and sly as they vied with one another in pursuit of the lovely life that was supposed to be theirs.

Some have divorced since then or died of accident or cancer or obscure degenerative disease, perhaps of slow despair.

Some have survived, stylish, anxious, and only occasionally rebarbative, following their men into the baffling octogenarian present. Aghast, they gaze in disbelief at the crumbling husks of the former prizes they were crowned for winning: the heartthrobs and the hunks, the college quarterbacks and the Phi Beta Kappas, who walk slowly, slowly at their sides, grateful to the sun for its warmth but too preoccupied, now, too engrossed in the hard work of decay, to bestow the myriad, minuscule sacramentals of wedlock. There are no more compliments on the new dress or hairdo, no chairs pulled out in restaurants, no car door protectively opened, no anniversary marked with a single, sweet-lipped rose. Their marriages, consummated in a heady time of terror, grew strong in the parched, glint-eyed famine of separation, but where has the potent young husband gone, with his broad, muscular chest, his medals, his orders and jokes, his immutable belief in his own calm vision, his imprint on the world? Who are these forgetful, stumbling strangers, their eyes dim, their soft tissue in disarray—hearts, lungs, brains, colons, prostates ignominiously throwing in the towel—who complain and bicker and thunderously lay down the law but cannot be relied upon in times of crisis to remember their own names? Bemused, the wives ponder the Do Not Resuscitate forms on file with their lawyers with copies in the permanent medical record and among the family's personal papers *(In the event of cardiac or respiratory arrest, no chest compressions, assisted ventilations, intubation, defibrillation, or cardiotonic medications),* the stern Advance Directives drawn up years ago when they were all immortal. They knew what love was, then. Is it still the same? And if it is, they wonder, where is it now?

ॐ   ॐ   ॐ

The doctors met when they were in their thirties, at last beginning their deferred clinical careers. World War II had just ended. Honed and disciplined, steady-eyed and secure in the habit of command, they had left the desolation of Europe, left the gaunt old world that had inhaled their youth and exhaled, like stale smoke, all the delicate webs that made up their understanding of themselves, and sailed safely home across a still dangerous ocean. Back in their own vast, penny-bright country, acknowledged as the heroes and miracle workers they had proved themselves to be, they began the task of shaping their post-war years. Unassailable, omniscient and glittering with competitive fire, they felt their power unchallenged. They hung out their shingles, attached themselves to hospitals, formed associations, forged new, professional friendships. They married the girls they either left behind or discovered on their odysseys; they bought houses in safe, leafy neighborhoods and started families. Ensconced, they basked serene as lizards under a benevolent sun, ruling their practices, their patients, and their families with the starry confidence of the anointed.

Nonetheless, experiences of the war burrowed beneath the rich loam of success like fluorescent earthworms. Sometimes, like earthworms surfacing to challenge the hard, beady gaze of a resolute bird, memories oozed up, mocking the authoritative young men and making them blanch and falter. Some felt the papery brush of Death's hand across their eyes; others stirred in their sleep and yearned for the dark ecstasy of the battlefield (so much more ineffable, it has been said, so much more astonishing and transcendent than the wild sunlit heights sometimes attained in the marriage bed), and felt sorrow and shame. Some reasoned that such raised scars on the spirit would surely fade, given time and the gentler domestic abrasions. Largely, though, the serpentine discomforts that lurked, uncoiled and restless, under their skins, or winked from the dregs of highball glasses or from the corners of brightly lit rooms, were either ignored or woven into the backgrounds of the immediate, evolving tapestries. There was so much to accomplish, so much to have, to hold, to taste and relish as the years slipped away.

榆 榆 榆

They are deep in their eighties now, best friends and colleagues who have aged and shared triumphs and disasters together. Over time, when called to do so and usually with no hard feelings, they have sat in stern professional judgment on one another. Now, as strength dissipates and disintegration creeps, they turn to each other for reassurance and are disappointed. Distracted, volatile, they draw the filaments of the Olympian imperatives born in medical school around shoulders—once so strong, so wide and reliable—that have grown arthritic and thin, just as their hands—oh, their faithful, knowledgeable hands!—have grown knotty and stiff, no longer to be trusted. Memory serves them gracelessly: they are fractious, inimical, certain that something has gone terribly wrong but reluctant to dwell on the discomfort long enough to name it. Indignantly, they summon habit and conviction to the lens of the ancient Hippocratic microscope.

But there is a malfunction in the gleaming apparatus. Overnight, some nameless mutation has smeared the slide. The indelible command that propelled them into the profession, that they saw spelled out through the sparse, attenuated years of medical school, that followed them into internship and residency and war service and that they believed engraved, not just on intellect but on muscle, bone, and tissue, is changing shape. Now, it appears, none of the Herculean tasks—the blistering education; the long, dedicated hours; the rigorous learning of new skills and honing of those already mastered; the meetings; the committees; the journals, studied and marked, clipped and filed, and studied again—is going to make one whit of difference.

Observing her guests, she recalls Samuel Beckett's remark that birth occurs astride of a grave. The man she married has spent his professional years peering through a microscope, avid for clues, intent on hunting down the killers that bring the stripped, silent corpses from the morgue. She came late to his life, but recognizes that he has built his career on the demand to know *why this happened;* for decades, teaching his students, guiding the continuing education of his colleagues, expounding in print, he has adamantly tried to make sense of the inexplicable. Lately he has read his own sentence in the appalling slides. Even so, his experience and expertise comfort him with the reminder that his own obliterating lightning will probably strike before the profligate cells consume his body. Nonetheless, he rejects the grim diagnosis handed down after chest pains place him in the emergency room. Affronted, he refuses the medication, cancels the appointment for the prescribed stress test. Burning-eyed, breathless, his nimbus of white hair ruffled around his head (like Einstein determined to outcoif Beethoven, she marvels), he wrenches a dog-eared textbook off the shelf and stabs his finger at the page, proclaiming his scornful discovery: *"Tietze's Syndrome! Hell's fire! Didn't I tell you? Right here in black and white—look!"*

She looks and sure enough, there it is, accurately describing all his symptoms: Tietze's, the great imposter, historical confounder of all cardiologists but, it appears, particularly baffling to this new breed of slapdash upstarts, these striplings untrained in differential diagnosis, who never use their hands but simply rely slavishly on their sophisticated machines. His younger colleagues, to whom he is still, after all this time, the Grand Old Man, are deferential but ruefully, unforgivingly insistent.

ؽ ؽ ؽ

Dying is a fact of life. But as if stalking the doctors were not insult enough, Death now stumbles preposterously upon their adult offspring, those who left home, made careers, married well, married disastrously, produced grandchildren, or chose not to procreate. Others, the ones who carelessly or accidentally died, have caused a profound disruption, for they found a gap in the heavily defended line and let the last enemy pass. When a physician's child dies, what happens is the dousing of light, a precipitous retreat into the chaos that existed before shape and logic emerged. For the wives, those deaths are emblems of all that is hellish, unimaginable. Their men were *doctors.* They probed the lacy strand that separates life from death with the skill of sandpipers at the edge of the tide; they were supposed to ensure that the void would not prevail, would not plunder their carefully constructed, richly embellished worlds.

Of course patients die, have always, arrogantly and perversely, died: these are professional failures to be regretted and grieved and ultimately forgiven. But for the doctors the injury-the insult, as they say about invasive procedures-that is happening now, that skewers the senses and splays the mind like a cadaver on an anatomist's bench, cannot be forgiven.

One is—he was—an oncologist. His only child has cancer. *"Do not intervene,"* he is told. *"We need the younger men, the wunderkinder, the ones with the newest knowledge, the latest techniques."* He has watched his desiccated child fade into a smudge of pale powder on a hospital pillow and he is mad with grief, Lear howling his never, never, nevers at an inattentive sky. His conversation rambles; he cannot concentrate enough to read; he curses the damnable genetic strength that backs up the injunction that took root when he was a student—*first do no harm!*—and binds him, making the ending of his life by his own hand an impossible escape. Another, a pediatrician, who lost one child to a drug overdose in a Las Vegas motel and a second to leukemia, has retreated into embarrassing sixties' fantasy: he sports sideburns and a groovy hairstyle, drives a jazzy sports car topdown in all weather, and relishes dangerous gymnastic sex with collagen-enhanced celebrity wannabes. To his peers, he is a figure of resigned, eye-rolling fun; he, in turn, pities their safe geriatric monogamy.

⚘ ⚘ ⚘

Old friends these old doctors may be, but they cannot shelter each other from these devastations. The exploding cannonball griefs that should draw them closer for comfort succeed only in alienating them from one another. They depress, bore, and infuriate each other. After each carefully spaced meeting, they telephone to complain about each other's failings. One, it is said, talks too slowly, pauses too often to chase down elusive connections, but then—remember the Surgery Committee meetings—didn't he always? One routinely offers the same critique of the fish soup in the waterfront restaurant: there is too much pepper in it today, or perhaps too little—for God's sake, is it too much to ask that they just get it right? Another calls, asking for news, anxious to appease a recent wrathful outburst during the course of which he told his beloved old friend that he was the worst goddamn driver in the history of powered transport and should not be permitted behind a wheel without an armored guard of outriders. Hanging up, the other sighs, bemusedly shakes his head and laments the dimming of his colleague's ability to recall any fact that is not somehow connected to World War II.

So now, Death waits at the edge of the shade for them, patient and amused, arms folded, counting the piling years, watching the treatments, the procedures, the pharmacopoeia, the midnight flights to the emergency room, all the feints and near misses. The revered healers, the hero warriors, cannot bear it. This cannot be happening. *They were the victors!* What went wrong? Who was the spy, the traitor, the snake in the grass? Who stole the maps, gave away the password, and sold them out?

❧   ❧   ❧

She watches. On the screen the music swells and recedes, the dancers give their all, the coveted golden men are handed out. The glittering movie stars, gorgeously appareled but evidently unable to believe the beneficence of fortune, gasp and weep as they accept their prizes. The stammered speeches of thanks unfurl and droop like banners on a windless day. In her living room, in front of the television, the beaches are still being stormed, the flag raised. The habits of command die hard; even during the Oscars the old doctors argue and jostle for control of the field.

"Hey, remember that number? *South Pacific.*"

"*South Pacific,* hell. It's *Guys and Dolls.*"

"Great number. Rita Hayworth sang it."

"*Dum dum dumdum / I could write a book / dum dum dum dum dum...*"

"Rita Hayworth wasn't in *Guys and Dolls.*"

"Right. That was *Pal Joey.*"

"*...dum dum walk and whistle and look....* Remember that?"

"Great song."

"Frank Sinatra, right?"

"Yeah, and Kim Hayes."

"You mean Holly Hayes."

"Right. She got an Oscar for *The Piano.*"

Death for them shall have no dominion—not while they remember the power they fought for and won and cannot relinquish.

Beside them, secretive and compliant, no longer wives but not yet widows, the women fall lightly, discreetly asleep.